LIGHTING FIRES
IN THE DARK

JONATHAN LIGGINS

flame
international

Published by Flame International
PO Box 424
Aldershot
Hampshire
GU11 9ER
UK

www.flameinternational.org

Published July 2015

British Library Cataloguing-in-Publication Data
A catalogue record for this book is available from the British Library.

ISBN: 978-0-9933428-0-6

Cover art and all photographs by Gareth Barton at www.bartoncreative.co.uk
Typesetting by www.zaccmedia.com
Printed in the United Kingdom

Contents

Foreword

I will place on his shoulder the
key to the house of David;
what he opens no one can shut,
and what he shuts no one can open.

(Isaiah 22:22)

There was a taxi waiting for me when my Heavenly Father miraculously led me out through the doors and gates of China's highest security prison early one morning. As I was sped away from that place I saw a key hanging from the driver's rear view mirror and the Lord spoke to me. "If I can release you from the solitary confinement of China's highest security prison," he declared, "then I can certainly release you from whatever is holding you. I hold the keys of David in my hands and the doors I open no man can close." I knew then that this was to be my message wherever I went and to this day I see my Lord releasing his children from the most binding of circumstances. It is the same for Flame International. They carry the same message of 'freedom for the captives'. Like me they know what it is to speak God's word into the dark places and to see his light shine in the hearts of men and women who have been crushed. Like me they have seen the Almighty move to restore broken hearts and bodies. Like me they have put aside human comfort to light the fire of God's love in the coldest of places. And like me they have lost much in order to serve the King of kings. Hallelujah!

I have travelled across the UK with these dear brothers and sisters in the Lord, working together for the sake of the Gospel. And with their help we have been able to place missionaries from the Chinese underground church into South Sudan – a place that Flame International know well – and we pray that these will be the first of many who will bring revival in that place and all the way back to Jerusalem. I know that this book will bless you and challenge you to join us as, together, we continue in our calling to 'light fires in the dark'.

Brother Yun
Frankfurt, May 2015

Author's Foreword

I have often wondered why almost every foreword features an appreciation of the writer's husband or wife. Now I know the answer. Having written this narrative, I realise what a time-consuming and all-absorbing task it is. So I want to start this book by thanking my wonderful wife, the Maggie Bradford, and latterly Maggie Liggins, mentioned and quoted at various points, for putting up with the innumerable hours my mind has been away from her. I want to thank her, too, for her encouragement in all sorts of ways.

I also want to thank the many people who have contributed to the writing of the book in one way or another. Maggie, however, has been crucial to it: if I had not met her at Morley Retreat House in Derbyshire in August 2006 I would not have heard of Flame International, still less become involved in it and write about it.

I was intrigued by what I heard about Flame in those few days at Morley. I hope that readers who have not previously heard about it will be similarly intrigued and that all readers will feel drawn into supporting its work in one way or another.

The book drew inspiration from Flame's tenth birthday party although I have not attempted to give a history of the organisation on a mission-by-mission basis. To do so would require a huge and unreadable tome. By describing some specific and particularly significant mission trips, I have tried to show the unusual things

Flame does and where it does them. By describing some of the major teachings, I have tried to show how the Lord has revitalised lives blighted by war or other devastating circumstances beyond their control. Finally, I have pointed up where Flame's ministry is likely to go in the second decade of its existence.

During the editing process, kindly undertaken in chief by Rosemary Piercy, I was encouraged by a conversation she had in a Plymouth coffee shop. She was reading a chapter of the book on her phone when a "glamorous lady" (Rosemary's words) took an adjacent seat. The lady asked what the book was about and, on hearing Rosemary's reply, opened up about her own traumatic past. A friendship was formed and their discussions continue. My sincere hope is that the book will be a catalyst for others to start on the road to Christian faith and to healing.

All biblical quotations are from the New International Version, unless otherwise stated. The book contains numerous individual quotes, some from people for whom English is not their mother tongue. I have not tried to clarify or interpret their words, still less to use the 'sic' formula often used in textbooks. What you read is precisely what the people have said. Likewise, I have not tried to update Thomas Hardy's language where I have quoted him in Chapter 6.

Jonathan Liggins,
Exmouth, Devon.
March, 2015.

BEGINNINGS

1

Celebration

*"He called his twelve disciples to him and gave them authority
to drive out evil spirits and to heal every disease and sickness"*
(Matthew 10:1)

**15ᵗʰ – 17ᵗʰ February 2013: Ashburnham Place, East Sussex,
England:**

It's party time. Ninety or so people have come together over a
beautiful, crisp winter weekend to celebrate Flame International's
tenth birthday. It has been a decade of missions to places far off the
tourist map, places where people have been massacred for no reason
other than belonging to a different tribe or having different ethnicity.
Flame has brought the Gospel of Peace, of forgiveness and of healing,
in the name of Jesus, into war-torn countries such as Sierra Leone,
Uganda, Rwanda, Burundi, South Sudan, the Democratic Republic
of Congo and the West Bank.

Women who have been raped; husbands or wives whose spouses
have been hacked to death in front of their eyes; parents who have
seen their sons kidnapped to be to turned into killing machines by
the Lord's Resistance Army, and their daughters abducted to become
either soldiers or sex slaves ('wives') for LRA soldiers; children who
have seen their parents, brothers and sisters brutally killed or who

have been forced to take part in the killings – all have one thing in common: their lives lie in ruins. They are deeply traumatised, bitter and in despair for the future. Real, in-depth, lasting healing has come to them as they have received the Gospel and teaching on subjects such as the interaction between body, soul and spirit, sin that spans the generations, and forgiveness. Broken bodies have been healed – the blind see, the dumb speak, the deaf hear and the lame walk. The greatest healing of all has been the coming to saving faith in Jesus of people of every age, colour and creed.

~

Jesus sent out 72 of his disciples on a training run in preparation for their later work with the words, *"When you enter a town...heal the sick who are there and tell them, 'The Kingdom of God is near you.'"* When these followers returned to base they reported, *"Lord, even the demons submit to us in your name."* They were full of joy – and small wonder! This has been Flame's experience too. The party was celebrating all that the Lord had done in bringing new life to so many hurting people, and looking ahead eagerly to the next decade.

It was a time of celebration – but much more than that. Flame has always encouraged its supporters to contribute to the strategic thinking behind the organization, so the weekend was an opportunity for them to do just that. They were able to provide suggestions and words about its direction that they believed to be from the Lord.

Many of them saw a need for Flame to complement its trauma healing work with practical aid. Was this to be direct, or by the setting up of a sister organisation, or by partnering with an existing aid agency? Was it to be by provision of food, clothing and medical supplies, or was it perhaps to be by provision of micro-finance to assist in the setting up of small businesses? Whatever, there were warnings against fostering the spirit of helplessness and dependency that the provision of aid often brings, and to guard against diluting Flame's core mission.

There were numerous words for specific places such as South Sudan, Burundi and the Democratic Republic of Congo, all encouraging an on-going involvement for Flame. People gave much food for thought, and cautious encouragement, to Flame's future role in China and the West Bank. There was much concern for Armenia, a country to which several preliminary visits had been made in order to assess what role Flame might play. Flame supporters saw it as a country at the intersection of Christian and Muslim influence; as the meeting point of different political ideologies; as a very needy place where Flame should rightly be involved. In fact, the autumn of 2013 would see the first full-scale mission to the country and more will be said about this in Chapter 14.

Another theme was that of Flame's pioneering work in its first decade and the consequent need that it should not allow itself to lapse into comfort zones in the second decade. Flame should therefore continue to make contacts in new places with a view to expanding God's healing ministry.

~

This book aims to show just what Jesus can achieve when his followers are faithful to his call to *"go out into the streets and alleys of the town and bring in the poor, the crippled, the blind and the lame"* (Luke 14:21). It is to show that even today, Jesus is in the business he announced to the people of Nazareth in their synagogue:

> *"The Spirit of the Lord is on me,*
> *because he has anointed me*
> *to proclaim good news to the poor.*
> *He has sent me to proclaim freedom for the prisoners*
> *and recovery of sight for the blind,*

to set the oppressed free,
to proclaim the year of the Lord's favour"

(Luke 4:18-19).

Last, but not least, it is to give some pointers to the development of Flame's work in years 10–20.

2

I just wanted to be of service…

*"Pretty amazing grace is what you showed me
Pretty amazing grace is who you are…"*

[Neil Diamond]

Those who know her today cannot believe that Jan Ransom – retired Lieutenant Colonel and now Chief Executive of Flame International – left school to study for a diploma in Domestic Science. Yet the story of Flame International cannot be separated from the story of its Chief Executive and no-one can chat to Jan for more than a couple of minutes without the conversation turning to Flame. The chances are that it will remain there no matter how long or short the meeting and no matter whether it is a formal business meeting or a dinner party. She is passionate about both the organisation and the God with whom it partners. Flame, not domestic science, was her destiny in the Lord and she is utterly focused on it.

Those who do not know Jan very well usually assume that she is effortlessly sociable from morning to night. In fact, she describes herself as a bit of a loner. This quality probably adds to her strength, as she copes with having to make decisions on which others can only advise. She is in fact a big thinker, a lady who sees the big picture of what God is doing, but who finds the detail tedious and relies on colleagues to deal with it. A text message is likely to require interpretation because Jan's mind has moved on to the next plan by the time she has finished the message.

Our God prepares his servants for their mission long before they come to know Jesus and before they become aware of what it is He wants them to do. It was certainly so with Jan. In her case she was within sight of her twenty-ninth birthday in 1983 when, as a result of a long letter from her former Commanding Officer (himself a committed Christian), she gave her life to the Lord. Everything changed from that point and her conversion put Jan on a path of radical discipleship. Up to then she had put 100% of herself into all she did. Now she wanted to be out and out for the Lord, with nothing less than all that He could give.

"I think I joined the army because I thought it would be exciting," says Jan. "I loved taking risks and the army offered me that opportunity. I am not sure I would have verbalised it like that when I was 21 years of age, but that is what I wanted. I think having an adrenaline rush was what challenged me about the Army." That readiness to take risks would certainly be significant in years to come.

Coming from a working-class background, she learned independence early in life as a result of having a father away at sea for long periods and a hard-working mother. After flirting with domestic science, she entered the Army, determined to be the best she could. This was at a time when women were only just being taken seriously as players in the armed forces. The result was a career in which Jan climbed high up the ladder, being awarded an MBE in Northern Ireland, and ending as a Lieutenant Colonel. To this day she has no clear idea, or (more likely) refuses to divulge, what led to the MBE.

In the Army Jan learned to lead but to do so in a gentle way, inspiring and encouraging rather than demanding and putting down. Macho-male culture was deeply engrained in the forces and, in dealing with the chauvinism and the hostility it created, she learned the forgiveness that has become a cornerstone of Flame's teaching. The result today is a leadership style that is quiet but firm, easy to follow, and that inspires confidence in those who join her teams.

Whilst stationed in the Falklands, just after she had become a Christian and in the immediate aftermath of the war with Argentina, she came face to face with grim living conditions. This was an excellent preparation for the conditions which Flame's teams have to live with during many of their missions – and not only those in Africa. Christian writer and broadcaster Michele Guinness, who came out of Jewish stock but married into the famous brewing family of that name, wrote a short biography of Jan. "There we were," she told Michele, "in very trying circumstances, living in makeshift portakabins without any of the basic creature comforts, driving around the utter desolation in vehicles the Argentinians had left behind."

Lack of an electricity supply has proved a feature of many Flame trips. Rosemary Piercy, who has been on many missions with Jan, comments that, "this poses a challenge for Jan since no electricity means no hair dryers. Many of us remember the sight of our leader appearing for early morning devotions, having commandeered her cylindrical hairbrush into the role of an outsize hair curler, so that the brush protrudes from one side of her hair like a miniature cannon. Many team members appear to think this is an absolutely normal part of the Flame experience".

Returning from the Falklands in 1984, Jan put to the test the missionary zeal she had felt since day one of her Christian journey. She wrote to numerous missionary societies offering herself for the mission field. All turned her down. "I think I realised the Lord had a mission field in the Army for me for a while. I was asked in 1994 to run the Ladies' Ministry in the Officers' Christian Union. I had a vision to see the ministry help women find healing, either in the armed forces or connected to it." It would be a ministry she carried out faithfully for fourteen years.

Her next posting, to Northern Ireland during the Troubles, taught her what it means to be part of a loving community. This came through attending a home group at Lisburn Cathedral. She began to learn how to make deep relationships even in the limited time Army postings give in one place. She learned, too, how to make herself vulnerable so that people could see, and relate to, the real Jan Ransom. "Army life has many virtues", says Jan, "but showing vulnerability is certainly not one of them."

The next big lesson was learning to love a diverse range of people, an ability that is essential in Flame's work. Jan was seconded to the Sultan of Brunei's forces. Her brief was to train 'Compani Askar Wanita', the Women's Company of the Royal Brunei Armed Forces. It was a unique posting in which she reported directly to the Colonel, who was none other than the Sultan's second wife. The three years she spent in Brunei were life-changing as she experienced what it was like for women living in a totally male-dominated culture. She learned to serve the women under her command and experienced a huge depth of relationships in return. "They were lovely, hard-working and honourable," she told Michele Guinness, "so easy to teach, with everything to strive for, so much more than in our society. I wanted them to have every opportunity I could give them."

Postings come and postings go in the armed forces, but leaving Brunei after three years left Jan bereft and rather resentful towards the Lord. She battled for a couple of years to come to terms with these feelings, really only managing this after being sent by the Army to the Chilwell Barracks in Nottingham. And it is at Chilwell that the story of Flame starts to take shape. "The adrenalin rush is just part and parcel of it, I get that and more working with Flame International. It is so exciting walking in the centre of the Lord's will."

At Chilwell she not only recognised the deeper, and often unperceived, purposes of God for her life but also learned to get what is now called the 'work-life balance' in perspective. Here, too, she met Maggie Bradford who would play a vital role in setting up Flame, be a trustee for its first decade and become a veteran of many Flame missions. Here also was where Jan started the women's ministry for the Officer's Christian Union, which inspired her thinking about how Flame should operate. And it was here that she had an encounter with the Holy Spirit, which, as she puts it, "started to give me vision."

The second weekend Jan organised for the Ladies' Ministry was a big learning point for her. It was to take place at Badger House – a country house a few miles from Bridgnorth in Shropshire – operated by the Cornelius Trust, which supports Christians in the armed forces. She had booked Pat Masterman to speak but six weeks before the conference was due to take place the Lord told Pat that she was not to attend. Jan searched in vain for a replacement.

The weekend arrived and only three ladies turned up for it. What was to be done? How was the weekend to be made worthwhile? "I had to ask the Lord constantly what was to be done next," Jan says. "He taught me that I had to rely on him on a moment-by-moment basis in this ministry. It was a learning experience and a hugely humbling one." It was a lesson that has provided the foundation for all Flame's missions. Humility is one of the key characteristics of Flame ministry.

But it was also in Chilwell that Jan was challenged to consider forgiveness. It turned her life around and teaching on this value has become a vital part of all Flame ministry. Jan recalls vividly the conversation with a male colleague: "Jan, do you like men?" he asked. "Yes, of course," she replied. "Well," said her colleague, "your behaviour doesn't indicate that." This sound bite was sufficient to make her realise that the male hostility towards women, which had seemed constant during her career, had caused reverse hostility on her part. "I would always verbally attack a man before he could attack me. I repented and chose to forgive men for what I considered to be abusive."

What was the result? "As I forgave, I was set free and I no longer believed the lie that all men hated me. I stopped attacking them. The bitterness and the hatred had gone."

~

14th February, 2002: It was time for Jan to leave the Army.

"The day I physically left the army was an extraordinary day. My entire army unit was on parade as I was driven out of the gates in a large truck – every soldier was lining the route and I felt very proud and very important."

Jan had left the Army – but had the Army left Jan?

"The next day, which was my 48th birthday", she says, "I flew to a women's conference called 'Deborah Arise' in Pensacola, Florida, with five friends. I was very expectant and excited! When we went to the first meeting my favourite worship leader, Lindall Cooley, was leading the worship. In a short while I felt the Lord nudge me to lie on the floor. I was obedient but as I lay there I realised that the Lord wasn't speaking to me. He was just letting me lie on the floor. There was a chorus sung called It's Time. I assumed it was time for me to get up...however I realised my legs were wobbly and had to lie down again."

Gabby Llewelyn was one of the friends with her. "Jan was determined to spend the whole week praising God – a great approach to a conference like this," she says. "Before I knew it Jan was face down on the floor. I thought, 'Oh, well, Jan is already engaging' so I rather left her to it, expecting it to be different the next day. But, no, as soon as the first prayer was prayed, the first chord played, down went Jan for the next few hours. It was a good conference for all of us but Jan spent virtually all the time flat on the floor, and very much sensing God's presence – though at the time none of us quite knew what was going on."

"My week was spent as a watchman", Gabby reflected. "We wanted to bring Jan back in one piece – humbled but not squashed!"

Jan recalled, "I had to lie on the floor for every session, and at no stage did the Lord speak. I just had to lie there. I spent over 10 hours on the floor flat on my face. Finally, as the conference was closing, the Lord said to me, 'That is where the mantle of my glory is revealed.' I realised I had to be humble and allow the Lieutenant Colonel to go out and the child of God to be developed!"

It was a pivotal moment in Jan's walk with the Lord. It was the beginning of the 'Year of Humbling.'

~

Further humbling came as a result of having to camp out for no less than seven weeks in order to secure the purchase of the ex-military, married-quarters house in which she now lives. Friends such as Maggie Bradford gave a helping hand. Of greater long-term significance, though, was the 40-day fast to which Jan felt a clear call immediately upon her return from Pensacola. There was no one who could give a helping hand with this.

Jan explains, "I had many people in my life who were sick. The call to fast had come five years earlier through reading a Mahesh Chavda book. I'd prayed regularly from then on that the Lord would prepare me, and when I returned from the conference the Lord told me to start. This was six months earlier than I thought I would do it."

Is she able to explain why the Lord called her to this extraordinary fast? "It's to do with humbling. Fasting is a humbling experience. You can't do it on your own for more than a day or two. I recognised that humility was going to be the basis on which Flame was founded. Jesus was the 'servant of all' and Flame teams have to be the same. As a result I believe I am called to fast regularly and I do it before most missions." Jan is quite clear; "Humility is a key for Flame International."

During those 40 days Jan settled down to start the six-month course at Ellel Ministries she had been planning to do before the fast. The 'NETS' (The Nine-Eleven Training School) course is based on Luke 9:11 *("He welcomed them and spoke to them about the kingdom of God, and healed those who needed healing"),* and covers the principles of Jesus' teaching on healing, deliverance and pastoral care. It not only confirmed the teaching that Jan had already embarked on with the ladies' ministry but it took her to a deeper level of understanding and revelation of it. "I personally had some significant healing during that time," says Jan.

About three weeks from the end of the course Jan had a further significant experience to prepare her for the work to come. "Jesus asked me, 'Are you prepared to die for me?' I spent three weeks wrestling with this question, weeping and seeking his face. On the final day of the course I said to the Lord, 'Yes, I am prepared to die for you.'" After that she received complete peace.

Ten hours spent on the floor at a conference; seven weeks camping out to secure a house; a forty-day fast; moving from significant commands in the Army to being a student on someone else's training course; accepting the possibility of death in the ministry she was to undertake. These all made a truly humbling season for Jan.

~

The scene was set. Jan's heart was right, she had the vision, she had the training, and she knew what the basic ministry would involve. As will become apparent, she also had the right team around her so that Flame International could become a reality. What she did not have, however, was clear direction about precisely to whom Flame was to minister and where. As the next chapter will show, that clarification was not long in coming.

~

Suggested further reading: The biography referred to is entitled *'Is God Good for Women?'* by Michelle Guinness and is published by Hodder & Stoughton. In it the author gives short biographies of a number of Christian women as she seeks to answer her own question.

3

Flames, Foundations and Traffic Lights

*"For this reason I remind you to **fan into flame** the gift of God, which is in you through the laying on of my hands."*

(2 Timothy 1:6)

Jerusalem AD 33: about 120 followers of Jesus are running scared and have locked themselves away in a top-floor room. Suddenly there is a sound which they could subsequently only describe as "the blowing of a violent wind" which filled the house. As if that were not enough, there appeared flames that separated and settled on the heads of everyone there. The running and the fear stopped. They marched boldly out of the room, into the street and preached to the huge and cosmopolitan crowd of people who had heard the commotion. The Church was born and never looked back.

Oxford, England 1554: In a very different way, flames played a major part in the reformation. These were the flames that burned people such as William Tyndale and the Oxford Martyrs, Hugh Latimer, Nicholas Ridley and Archbishop Thomas Cranmer. Latimer and Ridley met their horrible deaths in 1554 outside Balliol College, Latimer saying to Ridley the famous words, "Play the man, Master Ridley; we shall this day light such a candle, by God's grace, in England, as I trust shall never be put out". His prophecy has proved true.

It is perhaps no surprise then that Flame International's birth and development has been marked by prophecies and pictures of flames.

England 1994: Jan Ransom started the Ladies' Ministry for the Officers' Christian Union following her return from her tour of duty in the desolate Falklands. This was a ministry to women serving in the forces and the wives of serving officers. Although that ministry lasted 14 years there were early signs that it was only a stepping-stone. "Whilst I was running the Ladies Ministry," she comments, "we had a prophetic word that the ministry would be taken out to the nations and be like a flame lighting up the world." It was this prophecy that would give the charity its name when it came into being in 2003. To back it up, there would be a similar prophetic word in 2005, given through one of the trustees of Flame, who saw an Olympic torch being taken from nation to nation, spilling out flames as it went.

By 1998 Jan was starting to think more deeply of that wider ministry, one beyond the confines of the military. She was realising that there were an infinite number of people out there who needed the healing and reconciliation that she had pioneered amongst women in and around the armed forces. She started thinking of people who might partner her in the wider work, though her vision was still of taking healing to women only, with the area of operation being the Far East.

"I love the Far East! In my heart I always wanted to minister there. I suppose the climate and the intrigue and mystery attracted me," said Jan. "I had a great time whilst I was working with the Sultan of Brunei's armed forces and loved everything about it. I belonged to a predominantly Chinese church where I met many people who I really got on well with. I had Dr James Taylor, the great grandson of Hudson Taylor, come and speak in my apartment and I told him I wanted to be a missionary in China and the Far East. He told me I was already doing the job of a missionary."

Jan continued, "I also was given a supernatural love for the Chinese. I was on a flight to Singapore with very few Chinese on board, but every time one or two Chinese moved along the cabin I burst into tears, and I realised the Lord was giving me a love for this race."

The Lord usually takes us step by step in revealing his plan for our lives. Paul's Second Missionary Journey started with the limited aim of going back to the churches planted on the first journey to relay to them the decisions of the Council of Jerusalem, which are set down for posterity in Acts 15. It quickly developed into something much bigger. Having gone to the original churches, Paul and his companions found themselves unable to go back to Antioch in Syria. Instead, they were propelled westward into what is now Europe.

It became apparent that the Lord also had much broader plans for Flame International than those which Jan and her friends envisaged.

The following year, 1999, was particularly important for the developing vision. "Someone prophesised over me when I was Commanding Officer at Worthy Down," Jan says, "that I had been in the Army 'for such a time as this' and that the time was right for me to retire from army service." She spent the remaining three years of her command sharing her vision with those she wanted to join her in the enterprise – "selling it to them" in business terms – and setting up the group whose members would become founder-trustees of Flame International.

Not surprisingly, these were mostly women because the vision was still of an exclusively women's ministry. Gabby Llewellyn became Chair of the board of trustees. Says Jan, "I knew she understood the spiritual implications of the healing ministry. I trusted her discernment and wisdom and we started from there, operating out of my home."

But each trustee had a strategic role.

Maggie Bradford was "a really trusted friend, who had a heart for prayer ministry and was willing to take risks with me". Stephen Deakin "had a real heart and anointing for deliverance ministry and a prophetic gifting". Peck Lee was "Chinese and a very close friend who loved the ministry and, I saw, was significant for ministry in the Far East".

There was also Val Batchelor of whom Jan says, "I saw her come to the Lord and saw her desire for prayer ministry and the healing ministry". At about the time Flame was registered as a charity, Val was undergoing her own training and she would prove crucial to the organisation's development, leading numerous missions. "Without Val's huge support," says Jan, "the ministry would not have moved forward as it has."

These were to be the trustees of Flame upon its formation. They would be joined shortly afterwards by Katja Samuel who was "a very gifted lawyer and had a passion for the ministry".

Jan had finished her NETS training at Ellel Ministries and Maggie Bradford had completed similar training elsewhere. The pair then headed for Borneo and Sarawak, still envisaging that this would be the centre of activity. These areas had seen significant numbers of people converted, thanks largely to the activities of the Borneo Inland Mission under the power of the Holy Spirit.

There was a sense of expectancy as Jan spoke from Mark 2:1-12 on the healing of the man whose friends let him down through the roof of Jesus' house. She asked if the people hearing her were as desperate for healing as those friends had been. They were. There was a massive response, with most of the people attending coming forward for prayer for renewal and inner healing. The Spirit worked alongside to give healing from blindness, deafness, back and knee problems.

Significantly, two delegates had pictures of flames coming out of other people's heads, whilst one of them had a picture of a river running down from the platform. These pictures confirmed that

Flame was the right organisation at God's right time and that it carried his anointing.

Acts 16 recounts Paul's vision of the man from Macedonia beckoning. *"Come over to Macedonia and help us,"* said the nameless figure. And to Macedonia Paul willingly went. Flame's next development was also vision-driven and met with a similar whole-hearted response.

On a return flight from Malta with Maggie Bradford, Jan had a clear vision of a map of Africa. First it appeared in green, then in amber, and finally in red. It was not until sometime later that its significance became clear. She recounted the picture to a close friend, Joe Hawkey who, with his wife Ruth, would become pastors of Flame. Joe pointed out immediately that what she had seen was the traffic light sequence. He coupled it with a verse from John 8:35: *"Don't you have a saying, 'It's still four months until harvest'? I tell you, open your eyes and look at the fields! They are ripe for harvest."*

The message of the vision became apparent: Africa was where the Lord wanted Flame to concentrate its energies and the continent was ready for the ministry. However, it would not be the focus of the work indefinitely. It was clear that Africa, with its dreadful legacy of fighting, was the initial place for the ministry and it was to Africa that Flame went. China and the Far East would have to wait.

Within weeks a Flame team, with Jan Ransom as its leader, flew to Sierra Leone, a country recovering from a bitter civil war that had left an equally bitter legacy of broken people. This was the first of three missions to that country and resulted in valuable lessons for Flame as well as significant healing for the people reached by the conferences.

Stage three in the refining of the overall vision came about during that first Sierra Leone visit. Says Jan, "The purpose was modified after we had ministered to two hundred and fifty war widows in Sierra Leone, and the male chaplains asked why it was only the women who were receiving the ministry. 'Why', they asked, 'were the men in the church, military, police, prisons and government not receiving the teaching?"'

As a result Flame returned to minister to those people. "We realised," said Jan, "that teaching leaders was strategic and hence the change of direction."

The purpose had evolved from a ministry to women in the Far East to one including men, women and especially leaders in Africa. As will be seen, it also rapidly became a ministry to soldiers.

~

Suggested further reading: 'Drunk Before Dawn' by Shirley Lees (OMF Books) tells the story of the missionary work in Borneo that had been so successful.

4

What's So Special?

"For this reason I remind you to fan into flame the gift of God, which is in you through the laying on of my hands. For God did not give you a spirit of timidity, but a spirit of power, of love and of self-control."

2 Timothy 1: 6–7

Matthew Parris, well-known Times columnist of many years' standing, was born and brought up in Malawi, returning there in 2008, over forty years after he left it, to view the work of a small British aid charity. On 27th December 2008, as a result of what he saw, he published an article in the Times entitled "As an Atheist, I truly believe Africa needs God."

"Now a confirmed atheist," he wrote, "I've become convinced of the enormous contribution that Christian evangelism makes in Africa: sharply distinct from the work of secular NGOs, government projects and international aid efforts. These alone will not do. Education and training will not do. In Africa Christianity changes people's hearts. It brings a spiritual transformation. The rebirth is real. The change is good." He admitted quite freely that this was not a conclusion he wanted to reach but made it clear that his thoughts tied in with what he had seen and experienced years before both as a boy and a young man.

Flame International is totally committed to Christian evangelism – but not in a conventional way. If put as a typical multiple-choice question, asking what Flame International does, the choices might be:

- A missionary society
- An aid agency
- A Non-Governmental Organisation (NGO)
- None of the above

The answer would be the fourth – none of the above – because Flame's is a unique work fitting none of the recognised categories. It shares some characteristics of the first two whilst, on just one occasion, it registered for a time as an NGO. This was in Uganda and was for a specific purpose. It had applied for European Union funds to facilitate its trauma healing work in the country and registration was a pre-condition to the granting of money to any organisation. Sadly, despite the request to register having come from a Ugandan official who handled European funds, and despite one of Flame's trustees spending three complete weeks putting together the bid, nothing came of it. It is, just possibly, something that may bear fruit at some time in the future.

Flame believes strongly in the need for people to accept the salvation that Jesus brings and the abundant life that is part of it. Its teams regard themselves as "going on mission". The Gospel is always preached and people are urged to respond. "The Gospel," says Jan Ransom, "is the greatest form of healing." Bill Hybels, well-known Christian leader and Senior Pastor at Willow Creek Community Church in Chicago, speaks in similar terms. "We get to look for God's truest treasure, which is people," he says. "The greatest contribution you can make to anybody's life is an introduction to the God who loves them."

St. Paul said excitedly in 2 Corinthians 5:17 that: *"Therefore, if anyone is in Christ, the new creation has come: the old has gone, the new is here!"* Eugene Peterson, in his life-giving, modern translation puts it as: *"Now we look inside, and what we see is that anyone united with the Messiah gets a fresh start, is created new. The old life is gone; a new life burgeons!"* What both St. Paul and Eugene Paterson are saying is exactly what Matthew Parris has observed on the ground of Africa – in itself, the Gospel brings healing. It is life-giving.

But that is where the similarity to a missionary society stops. Flame's missions are short-term and it has no permanent presence in countries where it works.

On occasion Flame provides practical assistance: sewing machines to enable women to work; bikes to allow mobility; even a motorcycle to allow a bishop to get around his vast diocese. To this very limited extent it has the characteristic of an aid agency.

On occasion, too, Flame has been able to influence thinking in the House of Commons. Guildford MP, Anne Milton, mentioned concerns Flame had raised about the situation in the Nuba Mountains of South Sudan in a debate on Foreign affairs in the House of Commons on 23rd November 2009.

Part of Flame's uniqueness is in the combination it brings of preaching the gospel and prayer ministry for healing. Its work reflects the words of Isaiah:

> *"The Spirit of the Sovereign Lord is upon me because he has anointed me to preach good news to the poor. He has sent me to bind up the broken-hearted, to proclaim freedom for the captives and release from darkness for the prisoners, to proclaim the year of the Lord's favour...to comfort all who mourn...to bestow on them a crown of beauty instead of ashes, the oil of gladness instead of mourning, a garment of praise instead of a spirit of despair."*

Isaiah 61:1-4

These famous words, spoken at a time when many of the Jews were struggling to come to terms with exile in Babylonia, were later used by Jesus to describe his ministry. They have been a template for

Christians through the ages and describe exactly the work of Flame International.

It is worth repeating that Flame is virtually unique in the work it does. Its heart is for the hurting, for the broken, for the poorest, for those whose lives have been wrecked by war and oppression. Its first decade was spent mostly in ministering to the people of Africa, a continent that has seen more than its fair share of brutality, gruesome civil war and genocide. In just such countries Flame has worked: it is still working in most of them and the many people it has trained and healed are bringing healing to many others.

"Genocide" is a comparatively recent addition to the English language. Chambers Dictionary defines it as "the deliberate extermination of a racial, national, religious or ethnic group". In layman's terms it is the killing of a group of people for no reason other than their origin or beliefs. It was what Adolf Hitler tried to do to the Jews during, and in the years leading up to, World War II: the Holocaust.

"Trauma" is the word most often used to describe the effect of genocide on the survivors. "A trauma is an intensely painful emotional experience," wrote Christian psychologists Henry Cloud and John Townsend in their interesting book 'Boundaries.' They went on to say that, "The heart of God seems to beat especially close to the victim of trauma: 'He has sent me to bind up the broken-hearted' (Isaiah 61:1)".

And yet dictionary definitions, and even some psychologists' terms, do not bring over the real human horrors of genocide and trauma. Jan Ransom describes them in their real colours from first-hand experience over many years of ministry to victims. She says simply, "Brokenness. Jesus came to heal the broken. Many of the people we minister to have broken hearts. The consequences are things like inability to forgive; gut-wrenching fear and grief and sadness. Gut-wrenching is the word. Trauma has the effect of immobilising people. They are numb. They cannot show emotion. Everything is closed down."

Flame's Rosemary Piercy, who has considerable counselling experience, both secular and Christian, describes trauma as "a deep wounding, which is often beyond the reach of conventional counselling or prayer ministry. However, she goes on to say that, "When the time is right, we ask Jesus to reach down and release the trauma, and this leads, sometimes over a period of time, to full healing."

The infamous Lord's Resistance Army – the LRA – continues to be responsible for a huge amount of trauma as a result of its brutality. It has no clear aims and its soldiers owe allegiance to no one except themselves and the LRA's leader, Joseph Kony. Its activities make Kony one of the most wanted men in the world.

This private army kidnaps large numbers of children to turn them into child soldiers who will kill without compunction. For the girls, abduction is likely to mean becoming a sex slave to one of the senior soldiers. A few children manage to escape. For them, their experiences make it extremely difficult to settle back into family and village life. They may well have been forced by their abductors to kill family members or other villagers, so child, family and community members may need extensive ministry to make the change successfully.

Sierra Leone, Flame's first destination as a registered charity, saw 50,000 of its populace brutally murdered. Thousands of survivors lost both their homes and the communities in which they had once thrived. The 1994 genocide in Rwanda, taking place under the eye of the international community which did nothing to stop it, brought death to an estimated one million, mainly Tutsis but including many moderate Hutus who refused to take part in the massacre.

Sudan was at war with itself almost continuously from 1954 until the signing of the Comprehensive Peace Agreement in 2005. Flame's first mission to it came just a week after the signing of the treaty. The setting up in great hope and joy of the State of Southern Sudan in July 2011 has sadly seen a continuation of violence with the Islamic north bombing the people of the Nuba Mountains – the dividing line and buffer zone between the two states – whilst Southern Sudan has been at war with itself because of tribal antagonism.

Similar tragedies have occurred in Uganda, Burundi, the Republic of Congo and the Democratic Republic of Congo. And, in the midst of it all, the LRA has rampaged through the Democratic Republic of Congo, Uganda and Sudan.

All of these conflicts have brought the brokenness of trauma to huge numbers of people and, with it, the need for healing.

~

Not only is Flame's ministry to the broken but it also goes to areas where almost no one else goes. The remoteness of some locations can be gauged by the fact that, when a team first went into the remote Nuba Mountains, many of the people had rarely seen a white face. To gain access to these places Mission Aviation Fellowship's help is vital, with its fleet of light aircraft and skilled pilots. A glance at MAF's requirements on its website attests to the skills and experience it requires of its pilots.

Another unique feature of the charity lies in its teams spending time with the armed forces when on mission, ministering to war-weary and traumatised soldiers. Why the armed forces? Jan's answer is impressive, "The military are gatekeepers into the nation," she says. "They have authority, they have power and that power can be used in a godly way or an ungodly way. We've seen the ungodly in the Democratic Republic of Congo, where soldiers have gone and raped women under the authority of their Commanding Officer."

And, as if soldiers were not enough, at the end of missions teams make a point, where possible, of going to local prisons, ministering to men who are often in shackles. They visit hospitals regularly and preach in market places, providing a window to everyone for the Gospel.

~

Flame's trips are not without personal risk. Reflecting Jan Ransom's experience at the end of her Year of Humbling, one supporter, who has taken part in many Flame trips to Africa, said, "One of the things I have learnt when I go on a Flame trip is never to assume that I am coming home again. Flame does all that it can in taking reasonable precautions and in seeking the Lord. However, ultimately, when He gives a green light to go, team members need to go and not count the cost of what this might mean. This is a key to Flame fulfilling its mission and God-given potential, not least in the anticipation that spiritually darker days are yet to come."

Twice in the first ten years the trustees found it necessary to cancel missions as a result of particularly serious security situations. On one of these occasions the local bishop urged cancellation. The other was a mission that had been arranged to Malakal, a town in South Sudan lying on the banks of the White Nile and about four hundred miles north of the Republic's capital, Juba. This was in 2007 and Flame cancelled with extreme reluctance but under conviction that the Lord was clearly directing this.

The same team member commented that, "The days we live in are very urgent. Flame has a unique ministry to difficult and remote parts of the world. In some instances, the doors of opportunity are unlikely to remain open for long – so there is a real urgency to go if and when the Lord asks. However, it has to be at the right time, with the right prayer cover and other aspects put in place. There was a very sobering trustees meeting when the decision had to be taken to delay the planned trip to Malakal, as the necessary prayer cover was not in place. The Lord showed us that it was possible that not all of the team could come back if we went."

She continued, "However, we learnt through that too. The Lord is gracious and kind to those who are willing to go and do their best!"

The cancellation came about as a result of clear leading given to Gabby Llewelyn, who was Chair of the trustees at the time. "I had a huge check about the safety of the team going. It was not until the morning of the trustees' meeting when I was to share my thoughts with the trustees – I had already done so with Jan – that God gave me the scripture and confirmation in my mind that we did not have enough prayer cover for the trip. It was a very tough time for me as it was to be a strategic visit and many were disappointed but I knew for sure that God had halted it. People in my church had prayed and given very relevant pictures, having had no knowledge about what I was asking them to pray for. I still believe God kept us in Flame from some disaster in that season, and do not think we will know until we are in Glory what it was about, but good came out of it as it always does."

That good was very good. It was the birth of the Prayer Carpet, with Flame supporters promising one twelve hour 'shift' every month in order to provide 24/7 prayer cover. This has proved a massive blessing, particularly when a team is on mission, providing words, pictures, encouragement and warnings to the team by text or email.

But risk is often a present reality. In Burundi a man was shot dead right in front of the accommodation in which the team was staying. During one trip to southern Sudan there were dead bodies littering the streets of Malakal. There were further fatalities at a gathering in the local stadium when a riot broke out with tear gas being used to restore order.

16th October 2007 was another day of tension and one that the team in Juba, the capital of the new Republic of South Sudan, will not forget. Maggie Bradford, who by then was Maggie Liggins, recalls graphically, "On our last day we awoke to a curfew – no movement on the roads and the airport closed with the Army having cordoned off the town – and little hope of flying out. Apparently there had been an armed attack on the President's palace, and the Army was trying to track down the attackers and their weapons. As the morning progressed, we heard that two Eagle Air planes were landing. We saw a miracle unfold before our eyes. At 1 o'clock in the afternoon, with the bishop in his purple shirt in the front seat, we drove to the airport on an eerily quiet road, and managed to fly out as the airport had just opened. The Lord was sovereign in a very serious situation, although we felt safe throughout!"

~

Conditions in these African countries vary between uncomfortable and downright primitive, with food varying from poor to totally inedible. Fruit and vegetables are a luxury whilst goat is the staple meat.

Rats and insects are a regular problem, particularly at night. One team member devotes half a kilogram of her fifteen-kilo luggage allowance to anti-bug spray. Mosquito nets are a necessity, as is water purification equipment. Yet, in putting up with this, the team members are simply identifying with what their hosts have to cope with day-in and day-out.

"How do I cope with it?' mused another team member, 'My military background helps – I have done some pretty unpleasant things during military training and operations – humour, and God's grace in large measure!"

What are the rewards? Says one regular team member, "Witnessing change and healing in people's lives; the opportunity to teach; appreciation from delegates; travel." Another says, "It's an opportunity to change lives, including plundering the enemy's camp; it enriches our own lives; and puts our lives into better perspective – each time I come home to my flushing loo, hot shower, fridge and washing machine I think how I have no problems!"

One with no military background says the reward is, "connecting with great need in areas of suffering and trauma – and it's having an effect." Another speaks in similar terms, 'I love seeing God at work changing lives. I love encouraging brothers and sisters in Christ in a different culture and, hopefully, learning from them." Yet another comments, "It's the huge blessing of drawing alongside people who are eager to learn and to receive healing."

~

Flame's is a prayer ministry, though one grounded in teaching the truths of God's word as basis for healing and change. However, prayer ministry without background prayer is useless. "Prayer changes lives and potentially nations," says Jan. "Without prayer our ministry would be ineffective."

The 24/7 Prayer Carpet has become central to the operations but that is only one aspect of the bathing of the project in prayer.

There are annual prayer days held in Camberley and Crewe, whilst prayer groups meet regularly around the country. When a team is on mission its days start and end with times of prayer, and members of the team pray around the conference venue each day. Messages go back to Flame headquarters at the end of each day's ministry reporting on the progress of the conference, the points of praise and the prayer needs. These are relayed immediately to Flame's supporters, so that they can give thanks and intercede.

But has prayer worked? Is Jan justified in saying that without it the ministry would be ineffective? She would take us to Burundi to find an answer.

Matana, Burundi, 2013: The team is here at the Archbishop's invitation – it is their second visit. The conference is hard-going with the teaching seemingly hitting a brick wall. On the front row are the 'big men', the leaders of the church. They are sitting with arms folded in front of them, looking bored. It is obvious they are there under sufferance on the instructions of the Archbishop.

Jan takes up the story, "I was angry because we had spent money to get there and we as a team were putting in huge amounts of energy and time. At the end of the day we went back to the guesthouse. I sent home a text message to our prayer supporters that we needed breakthrough with the 'big men'. As a team we prayed for breakthrough and warfared for it to come. I was still quite cross about their attitude and their pride."

It was the following morning, before the conference started, that things began to change. "I was reading 1 Corinthians 4:12-13, which says *'When we are cursed we bless, when we are persecuted, we endure it, when we are slandered, we answer kindly.'* I realised it was my attitude that needed breakthrough as I was not loving them they way I ought to have been. So I repented to the team and asked for forgiveness and asked the whole team to show extravagant love. We did just that and I went along the front row giving huge hugs. We just continued to show love and the Lord broke through into their lives!"

At the end of the conference the first and most influential man confessed that his and his family's life had been changed. Another said he would ensure that what had been said and done was taught at the local bible school, and many more spoke about transformed lives. Along the way Jan and the team had learned a valuable lesson, which she puts in this way, "We have to make sure our lives are aligned to the word of God and not to judge others! As we give extravagant love, Almighty God is able to melt even the most hardened hearts. May we always be teachable and always willing to be humble".

This story shows the sequence of prayer: a difficult situation forced the team and supporters to pray; the Lord's answer was to show the team leader that her attitudes were wrong; she, in turn, was able to repent and lead the team into a better, godly way of dealing with the people who were difficult; they responded; the barriers came down.

Jan Ransom sums up the powerful effect of prayer, "Constant prayer on our behalf has helped us to maintain an anointed ministry wherever we go. Without this prayer it would have been an even greater struggle than we experience. The ministry is always contested by the enemy, but prayer limits the effectiveness of Satan."

~

Flame works with people who are often very deeply wounded in their souls and spirits because of the horrors of violence and oppression.

They live with a sense of hopelessness and bitterness. Moreover, in Africa, where witchcraft is endemic, people are at the mercy of both witchdoctors and curses. Even when they become Christians, they often return to the local witchdoctor because of the lack of any proper health care. In addition, many have similar problems to those faced in the western world: the results of bad parenting, absent fathers and poverty. Many African children resent their families, because lack of finance has curtailed their education and therefore their chance to escape the cycle of deprivation.

The problems are deep. Flame's experience time after time is that the Lord is not only equal to all these problems but more than conqueror. The prayer ministry, however, needs to be as deep as the problems themselves, so Flame aims to go to the roots.

The ministry is, on the one hand, a teaching one and, on the other, a prayer ministry. The two go together. Prayer ministry is often done in small groups, with one or two team members facilitating and encouraging the delegates to minister to one another. In this way they are trained to take on the healing ministry in their own communities. This builds on the teachings given, which are the keys to unearthing the roots of the problems delegates face. Much of the prayer is by the delegates themselves, first sharing the problem with other group members then confessing their own part in it – lack of forgiveness, bitterness, dabbling in the occult for example – and then asking the Lord for the healing they want, and which he longs to give them.

The teaching is wide-ranging: many would describe it as cutting-edge. It is built on Flame's experience of what lies behind the continued problems and suffering of humankind. There is almost always the teaching on truth and lies whilst through the teaching on body, soul and spirit, delegates are encouraged to see how problems in one area have a knock-on effect on the others. One member of the 2013 Armenia team said, "We noticed that there were an unusual number of people with pains in the neck, back and joints. And it soon became apparent that the root cause was the spiritual and emotional oppression of the communist regime they had lived under for so many years. As the teaching sessions progressed many of these physical pains simply disappeared as people experienced freedom from the past".

Teams encourage delegates to look at their family history to see if what they are doing is a repeat of what previous generations have done. If it is, they will also be encouraged to repent of their own part in it, so as to break the cycle of negative behaviour in the present. In addition to this, there may be teaching to highlight the unhelpful emotional and spiritual bonds that exist between people and which need breaking if there is to be true freedom and healing. Much honesty and courage is required for this, so the making of good relationships between team and delegates is vital in order to build a high level of trust.

Teaching on forgiveness is also vital. It is the prime key to receiving God's blessing, to releasing bitterness and to the reconciliation between people of differing tribal backgrounds, which is needed for peace.

Fear is a major factor in human behaviour. In Jan Ransom's experience it is "the biggest driver of human behaviour." Matthew Parris, in his Times article, said, "Anxiety – fear of evil spirits, of ancestors, of nature and the wild, of tribal hierarchy, of quite everyday things – strikes deep into the whole structure of rural African thought. Every man has his place and, call it fear or respect, a great weight grinds down the individual spirit, stunting curiosity." So enabling delegates to walk free of it, assured of the love of their Heavenly Father, is another vital ingredient of healing.

The teaching is essential to the prayer that is at the heart of the healing ministry. The question is: how do you effectively get across the teaching, especially when the delegates are non-English speakers? This is almost always the case. Good translators are a prime requirement – and Flame's teams have been blessed with very capable ones. However, words are only a minor part of communication, which means that non-verbal communication, including facial expression and body language, is necessary to teach fully. Flame's solution, which seems to cut across all cultures, is the use of drama. It is served up with the use of basic props and a large dose of humour: the old English proverb that "laughter is the best medicine" has backing from Scripture.

The essence of all the dramas is simplicity. The team acts out the forgiveness teaching of the Parable of the Unmerciful Servant of Matthew 18:21-35, using a crown and gown for the king and a fold-up, hand-held cloth latticework for the prison. The use of drama breaks down barriers between the team and delegates, as the team members show their willingness to make fools of themselves, and everyone laughs together. The delegates can easily replicate the dramas and props when they take the teachings back to their communities. Invariably delegates catch on to the meaning of the teaching very quickly.

The primary prop is always a cross at the front. When asking delegates to forgive, the team provides a hammer, nails and red paper discs. Delegates come out and nail a disc to the cross to symbolise publically that they have forgiven a particular person or offence. Often someone will nail several discs to the cross, acknowledging that they have much to forgive. Occasionally teams use small stones instead of the paper discs and delegates lay a stone at the cross. The effect is the same. No matter what else is taught, this is always a powerful moment in the conferences and a turning point for many of the delegates.

~

"It is significant that our project work in Sierra Leone has centred on healing men and women damaged by the atrocities of war and on reconciliation. Reconciliation through forgiveness is emerging as the backbone of the missionary work, with the emphasis on ministering to war widows and women's groups. This has led to training male Pastors and Leaders. Our focus will remain on the spiritual healing of hurting men and women."

So says Flame's 2005 Annual Report. The significance of the words is in indicating Flame's approach to ministry: not only the centrality of forgiveness but also the need to train pastors and leaders who, in turn, can then take the ministry to others. Jesus quickly realised that he could not do it all by himself so he set about gathering and training a bunch of followers from which the apostles emerged. "One man shall tell another and another shall tell his friend," describes the New Testament way of spreading the gospel. The need is enormous and only by ministering to key people, and them passing on the ministry to others, can that need be met.

Bishop Samuel Peni of Nzara Diocese in Sudan, whose testimony to the efficacy of the Flame work is set out at the end of this chapter, said that one hundred and twenty of his clergy and church leaders had attended Flame conferences. Of these, forty had trained others but all had ministered in some way to others. As a result, "Over 20,000 people in the diocese of Nzara have been impacted in one way or another".

This is a measure of the impact of Flame – and it can be multiplied diocese by diocese and country-by-country in which the charity has worked.

Testimony of Bishop Samuel Peni of Nzara, South Sudan, sent to Flame on 27th May 2013

Greetings to you in Jesus name.

This is to inform you that the teachings you passed to us are now taking root among our people in Ezo.

Since Friday last week a team of our evangelists including me, the Principal of our diocesan Bible School, the pastors of that Archdeaconry, Mothers' union leaders and members, youth leaders and their members, Sunday school teachers and over 300 children gathered at the ECS St. Mark church in Baragu area, eighteen miles away from the diocesan centre.

The purpose was to give a two-day workshop on:

35

1. *Unity and Disunity.*
2. *Love.*
3. *Our enemy Satan, the world and our body.*
4. *Harmful traditional practices.*
5. *Teaching for Sunday school children.*
6. *Teaching on evangelism and mission.*

These teaching sessions were attended by three popular Roman Catholic churches in the area. Also local chiefs, sub-chiefs, headmen and government officials attended because they were grateful to hear us talking of unity and removal of harmful traditional practices, which exist among their community. After the first day teachings many people who possess witchcraft* brought them to us in the church. Some well-known figures in those practices, who wanted to hide and still continue, were followed by the chiefs and evangelists who removed their witchcrafts* and took them to the church compound for burning after some powerful brief prayer. Christians were marching round these collected witchcrafts* singing praises in victory to the Lord before they were burnt.

In the report presented by our evangelism team leader, 146 people had been healed from various sicknesses. Five people who could not see well can now see very well. One paralysed man, who was bewitched and could not walk or hold something for four years, got up and walked. He danced for many hours in our Sunday worship. Womb problems in women and casting out of evil spirits were the major sicknesses. One young man was healed, who had taken powers from evil spirits at the source of a river and stayed with it for 13 years. He had been bitten many times by poisonous snakes as punishment whenever he went against the spirits' instructions. These evil spirits instructed him not to eat fish all his life but after the Lord delivered him we gave him a cooked fish to eat and he ate without any problem. People were surprised and again, grateful to hear their living testimonies as they stood before the crowds at worship on Sunday.

*The Bishop is referring to items used in witchcraft

Suggested Further Reading: The fascinating story of the origins and development of Mission Aviation Fellowship – MAF - is told in Stuart King's book 'Hope has Wings: the Mission Aviation Fellowship Story' by Stuart King. MAF and Flame enjoy a fruitful relationship.

INTO ACTION

5

A Steep Learning Curve: Sierra Leone

"The first evening we were in Sierra Leone we travelled from the ferry, to where we were staying, in a four-wheel drive truck. Maybe it was because it was my first experience of Africa but what struck me was the darkness. It was not threatening, just very dark. It was also very quiet. And every so often there was the soft light of a small cooking fire in one of the roadside homes. Although it was a typical warm African night and the month was June, what came strongly to mind for me was the carol, "O Little Town of Bethlehem", and particularly the line, "Yet in thy dark streets shineth, the everlasting light. The hopes and fears of all the years are met in thee tonight". Whatever the hopes and fears of the people living there, they could all be met in Jesus Christ."

[Maggie Bradford - member of the Flame team,

Sierra Leone, June 2003]

"Go", said Jesus, "your faith has healed you." Immediately he [Bartimaeus] received his sight and followed Jesus along the road."

(Mark 10:52)

Like most civil wars, the fighting in Sierra Leone was marked by atrocities. This "Land of the Freed Men" became the land of the traumatised, with fifty thousand people dead and many hundreds of thousands displaced. Very many had fled to neighbouring countries such as Guinea and Liberia.

On 16th June 2003 a Flame team led by Jan Ransom left England for Sierra Leone to minister to two hundred and fifty hurting widows. This proved to be the first of three missions to that country over the next three years. They were going to a battle-scarred country where the civil war had ended less than two years previously.

Modern Sierra Leone has its roots in the settlement in 1792 of nearly twelve hundred Afro-American slaves, most of whom had escaped to Nova Scotia from plantations in Virginia and the Carolinas. It became a British Colony and Protectorate, achieving independence on 6th April 1961. The initial years boded well for the new nation but corruption and both political and ethnic rivalry soon took their toll. There were three military coups. In 1991 the formation of the R.U.F (the Revolutionary United Front), with support from the notorious Liberian rebel leader, Charles Taylor, led to full-scale civil war. By 1999 the situation was so grave that the United Nations sent in peacekeepers whose numbers quickly rose from six thousand to eleven thousand. In 2001 the British Army launched a major offensive against the RUF. This action brought the defeat of the RUF and restored both peace and democracy. The end of the conflict was announced officially in January 2002.

Though the fighting may have finished, civil wars such as this leave a nation of people in deep distress and confusion. These after-effects do not easily or quickly disappear. It is to these victims that Flame takes its ministry – though the purpose of this first trip was limited to holding a healing conference only for the war widows.

The mission had its origins in Nigeria, which had provided peacekeepers for Liberia in the 1980's. These troops had been Charles Taylor's target in inspiring the setting up of the RUF. In early 2003 Jan Ransom and Val Batchelor, a former brigadier in the British army, were at a military conference in Lagos. Jan was to give the last talk of the day but it was steamy hot, there had been no lunch break nor had anyone eaten. She was to speak on forgiveness to an audience of about 30 women, mostly the wives of serving Nigerian Army personnel, with four other seminars due to take place in the same room at the same time. "I had problems with my words, problems finding appropriate scriptures and problems with translators. It was probably the worst talk I've ever given," she says.

Val recalls the two of them going back to their guesthouse feeling thoroughly gloomy. "It looked grim," she comments, "so we really felt the need to pray about it, asking the Lord to bring fruit despite what had gone on." There was a knock at their door and two people came in – Moses Kargbo, the Senior Chaplain to the Sierra Leone Army, and his wife, Juliette. Moses came to the point of the visit quickly and bluntly, "Our widows need that teaching. Will you come to Sierra Leone?"

The Lord was bringing fruit, opening a door even though in human terms Jan's talk had been a disaster. Flame grasped firmly the opportunity presented by the Lord and this first mission to Sierra Leone was the result.

~

The drive from Lungi Airport gave a taste of the problems faced by the country: along the roadside there were graves and sweet potato plantings in equal measure, symbolising the country's recent conflict and its present struggle to re-establish itself. Freetown, Sierra Leone's capital, was at that time the only capital city in the world to have no electricity. Crossing the river dividing Freetown from the airport on the crowded Lungi ferry, the team noticed the hulks of sunken boats, all victims of the vicious fighting so recently ended. It transpired that many of the delegates for the conference were travelling on the ferry.

The team's accommodation (as they discovered after the conference) had previously been used as a brothel. The women, however, had been moved out and some of the red lights replaced by white ones, though one team member described the furnishings as "still somewhat unusual". The accommodation was basic, to say the least, but even here there was an early lesson for Flame. "Please," asked co-host Henry Ladele, "join in our hardships without grumbling, complaining or criticising". That has been a watchword for Flame International for its many subsequent missions. "Mission teams need to go with servant-hearts and hearts grateful for whatever conditions are like. On occasions, this is hard," says Jan.

The conference itself started on the Wednesday, with opening worship during which a number of evil spirits manifested, as indeed they did during several later worship sessions. Henry Ladele spoke on the healing of Blind Bartimaeus, declaring that no one can encounter Jesus and remain the same. This created a sense of expectancy among the delegates.

There followed a session on what we believe as Christians. Flame's experience is that it is vital for the healing process to deal with thought systems which are often deeply entrenched in the thinking of the local people, but which are contrary to the Gospel. In Africa witchdoctors and witchcraft are at the root of belief systems and, even where Christianity is widely accepted, there is a large degree of syncretism of old thinking with the new. These lies have to be brought to the surface and challenged if people are to experience the "freedom we have in Christ".

The confusion in belief systems was graphically illustrated by the experience of one delegate who we will call Anna, though that was not her real name. The incident seems bizarre to western ears and may have been an example of "sympathetic magic," which is a ritual intended to bring about what it signifies, rather like the making of an effigy of a person and the sticking of a pin in it to bring about death. During the civil war there had been instances of people being buried alive and Anna told how, despite being Roman Catholic, she had been laid in a grave and partially covered in soil. She said that she could do nothing about it: she may well have been ordered to do it by her parents and in that culture she would obey without question. A fire had been lit on top of the soil and she had been told that she must repeat the Lord's Prayer. Anna did this and was then lifted out of the grave, apparently uninjured. The intention may have been to bring new life out of the old, though this is speculative.

Whatever the truth about Anna's experience, about 30 people came forward for prayer and to commit their lives to Jesus that day. One of these was Edna, a Muslim who had been one of the women on the Freetown to Lungi ferry. She told her story later, "I was on the ferry with my baby. I intended to make my way to the Liberian frontier. I wanted to kill myself by getting in the middle of the fighting going on there". But the Lord had other purposes for Edna and her child. "On the ferry I met some of the Christian women going to the conference and they persuaded me to come too. Now I have accepted Jesus," she said happily. One of the other women at the conference took Edna into her own home.

It quickly became apparent that the Sierra Leonean people were living in fear. Rosemary Piercy described it as "probably the strongest emotion we found on that unforgettable first trip to Sierra Leone". By way of explanation she says, "Almost every lady seemed to be fearful of a 'bush spirit', which was a spirit they believed lived only in the wilds, and which would assail them if they went far out into the bush. It appeared to be the personification of fear. The fear also shown by one or two people, as they confessed their involvement in ungodly rituals, was so strong that they found it almost impossible to speak. Fear is indeed the principal and highly successful weapon of the enemy."

As the conference progressed, the team taught on the connection between body, soul and spirit, on family tendencies to particular sins, on godly sex and on forgiveness. At the end of it fifteen more women accepted Jesus as saviour. A number testified to the healing they had received as a result of the small-group workshops that the team conducted in conjunction with the teaching.

One lady had come forward after the forgiveness teaching to hammer a red disc into the cross. "I was forgiving my neighbour," she testified later. "I went home afterwards and told my neighbour what I had done. I asked her to come to the conference the next day. We came together." The neighbour gave her life to Jesus.

Mary, who had many old scars from cuts on her face, and a chronic cough and sickness, was looking transformed when she appeared at the church service on the final Sunday. Agnes brought her two-year old daughter because of sickness and lameness. The following day the child was seen walking.

Rosemary Piercy recalls another vivid incident. Agatha (again not her real name) had come running up for prayer at the end of the first session asking, as did many other ladies, to be delivered from the 'bush spirit'. Said Rosemary, "We explained that often we have to forgive our enemies and receive healing from the effects of both generational influences and also traumatic events in our own lives before we can receive lasting deliverance. She was sceptical and obviously doubted our abilities to pray." However, as the conference progressed, Agatha and many others were freed, not only from the bush spirit (whatever it precisely may have been), but also from a variety of chest and stomach disorders.

Significantly for the future, Jan was realising as the conference progressed that it was not just women who had suffered and were traumatised by war. The story has already been told of the puzzled reaction of the chaplains to the women-only approach. The open doors of the church were filled by men who were asking why they too could not receive healing. At another church visited by the team the verger was a soldier who had had part of his face blown off in the war and who was now working full-time for the church. He was obviously in need of healing.

It became clear that Flame must broaden its outlook so that everyone affected could have the opportunity to receive teaching and ministry. This, though, was by no means the only lesson for Flame from the visit. The team had come to terms with the need to accept local conditions without quibble. This had a lasting legacy, but Rosemary Piercy commented on two other significant pieces of learning. "A valuable lesson learned from that first trip was that if we minister to people immediately after a traumatic event it is sometimes just not possible for them to respond to the teaching and the prayer; their emotions are still too raw to be faced. We also faced a cultural reluctance to admit negative emotions; this was the first, and by no means the last, time that we came up against this challenge."

~

In May 2004 Flame returned to Sierra Leone to continue the healing ministry, but this time to help both men and women. Towards the end of the first visit the team became aware that a group of local intercessors was praying fervently for their country and were so dedicated that many of them worked for most of the day then prayed unceasingly throughout the night. Rosemary commented that, "This was one of the many humbling experiences that Flame teams have had, and it is significant that we were able to have so much local support. When we returned for the second visit we had noticed immediately that the atmosphere over the country was less oppressive. Whatever the reason for this, we were grateful to the Lord for his intervention."

Among the many messages from Flame's prayer supporters at the beginning of the second mission was one from Sheffield, which seemed to bear out the changes the team noticed and to justify the intercessors' prayers:

> "I saw a vision of you all boarding a plane, and with you, you took many sacks of wheat. Also, there were two big water jars, and these were full of water. On the side of the jars it said 'Living Water'. I believe the interpretation to this vision is that you will feed the people with the wheat in whatever you are taking with you (sermons, prayers, ministry and each one of your gifts). I also feel that the jars are Jesus, and as Jesus said, 'Whoever drinks of this water will never be thirsty again.' I believe this is for new believers and to fill people ministered to last time with God's Living Water. I am reminded of the scriptures of the woman who

47

went to the well and spoke to Jesus, in John 4:11-16. I feel that as you minister to these people they will have a transforming experience, just like the woman at the well."

The pastor of the Church where the previous year's conference had been held told of the living water brought by the 2003 Flame ministry. "The women of my church have been changed by the conference last year," he said. "They had been in despair but now their faith has been revived and they have started up a tie-dyeing business."

The beginning of the conference was marred by the deaths of four delegates in a car crash on their way there. This was an "incredible dampener," as a team member described it. And yet the blessing continued with two hundred and twenty delegates, including the wife of the Ghanaian Ambassador. One delegate, Rosalind, had been forced to watch the killing of her husband and the burning of his body. She received life-giving ministry.

Flame's teaching on forgiveness, which is described in more detail in chapter 7, proved very powerful. Maggie Bradford recalled, "Moses – one of the team's hosts – led the way, hammering a red disc onto one of the crosses. Two had been made for us and arrived in the nick of time. About a hundred people came up to the crosses, some writing the names of people on their red discs".

But this conference was auspicious, not just because Flame's horizons broadened to encompass men, but because of the time spent with the Army, something for which Flame is uniquely equipped. Even before the conference started the team had spent time at Army Headquarters as a result of relationships with two Christians, Brigadier Nelson Williams, the Deputy Chief of the Defence Staff, and Major General Edwin Sam Mbomah. Major General Mbomah opened the conference, saying that Christian men and women in the armed forces of Sierra Leone could change the nation.

Ministry to the armed forces, wherever teams go, has become a major part of Flame's work and will be the subject of chapter 12.

~

In June 2006 Jan led another team to Sierra Leone at the invitation of a Sierra Leonean pastor, Arnold Anthony. This time they went to the town of Kenema, which is the third largest city in the country, lying 185 miles south-east of Freetown, with an ethnically diverse population of nearly 190,000. Arnold had asked Flame to bring a number of seriously extra large T-shirts in the standard Flame bottle-green colour and with the Flame logo printed on them. He took the team to meet the town's headmen, who were Muslims and who were to be the recipients of the shirts, which turned out to be in their tribal colour. They were delighted. It transpired that the Chief Headman had a nephew who was a Pentecostal pastor in the town. He announced to Jan, "You have my authority to do whatever the Lord has called you to do in this town".

"We found out that the townsfolk's ancestors had covenanted the land on which it was built to the powers of darkness," says Jan. "There had been much blood shed on it since and in the most horrible ways imaginable." Soldiers, it seemed, would bet on the sex of a child in the womb and then slice open the woman's womb to see who had won. Other soldiers had pushed tyres over victims, and set them on fire.

The conference culminated in a communion service, celebrating the new covenant established by Jesus as a result of his death and resurrection. Key local leaders –military, church and municipal – took part in this simple service. They confessed the sin of their ancestors in establishing the old covenant with the powers of darkness, renounced it and so broke the curses on the land that had come with it. "They used the new covenant with Jesus to show their dissatisfaction with the old one," commented Jan afterwards.

As the conference progressed a local prince asked the team to visit his village. This involved a six-hour detour along what appeared to be a dried-up river bed. The journey, however, was well worth it, since after Jan's brief talk, every person in the village put up their hands to receive Jesus. The more sceptical members of the team were eventually put in their place with news a year later that the village had been completely transformed.

The following day an excited Pastor Arnold spoke to the team, "God spoke to me last night. He said that the prophecies he had given me fifteen years ago have been fulfilled through this mission. I'm amazed that this was done through a bunch of old white women".

Flame's direct involvement with Sierra Leone ended with this conference but its legacy lives on with the teaching being taken out by the delegates to their homes and churches. For Flame there had been a number of lessons, not least of which was an understanding of the powers of darkness and of cleansing the land itself, as well as bringing healing to the people.

6

Like father, like son...

"I began to worry, a little later, that the sins my captors had sown in me were being harvested in my family in more ways than one. Among Far Eastern ex-prisoners-of-war there is a rumbling of belief that our children are damaged, in some way genetically harmed. It seems to us, when we get together now as older men, that we have bequeathed some strange problems to our children."

[Eric Lomax: "The Railway Man"
Page 222]

"...visiting the iniquity of the fathers on the children to the third and fourth generations..."

(Exodus 20:5)

"After hearing the teaching I was very excited. I went back to my own church and preached about it. Six people came forward for baptism as a result."

[A Pastor at the Flame Kajo Keji Conference
in September 2009]

The whole family was at it. Dad told lies, his son told lies and so did his grandson. In Abraham's family it just seemed that lying was a way of life.

When it suited him, to save his skin, Pop Abraham was quite happy to make his wife tell lies about their relationship, even if it meant her ending up in another guy's harem. As long as Abraham was all right her wellbeing didn't seem to matter. And anyway, she was his half-sister...

Son Isaac was quite happy to play the same trick on Abimelech. Later, Isaac was the victim of an audacious deception by his wife, Rebekah, and his second son, Jacob, which resulted in Jacob getting the blessing his older brother should have had. Perhaps Rebekah was taking her opportunity to get one back at her husband, once his poor health gave her the upper hand in their relationship?

As for Jacob, he both deceived and was deceived. Stealing the blessing gave him no option but to flee from his brother Esau. He ended up living with his Uncle Laban, Rebekah's brother. Jacob worked seven years for Laban on the promise of receiving his uncle's lovely younger daughter, Rachel, in marriage. Laban himself was not above a spot of deception and so, seven years on, Jacob found he had married the much less attractive older daughter, Leah. "Well, the younger couldn't marry before the elder, could she?" reasoned Laban.

And so Jacob put in another seven years of shepherding as the bride-price for Rachel. Along the way there was deception and counter-deception between Laban and Jacob over the sheep. Lying had almost become a family game: you can read the whole sorry tale in full in Genesis 12 verse 10 to the end of Genesis chapter 31.

It seems that behaviour patterns have a habit of passing from one generation to another. Godly traits in one generation often appear in the next. On the other hand ungodly, and often destructive, traits also appear in following generations. Abused children sadly may become abusers. Children from broken homes may find themselves in broken relationships. Addictions in one generation recur in the next. "He's just like his father," is often heard. "Her mother did exactly the same." It is too frequent to be co-incidence. It is not inevitable but we are seemingly prone to acting out the same behaviour patterns that our forebears did. We are each likely to get caught up in certain negative behaviour patterns more than in others.

In his novel 'Far from the Madding Crowd' Thomas Hardy has his characters Gabriel Oak and Bathsheba discussing how poor Cain Ball got his unfortunate forename. "Oh you see, mem," says Gabriel, "his pore mother, not being a scripture-read woman, made a mistake at his christening, thinking 'twas Abel killed Cain, and called en Cain, meaning Abel all the time. The Parson put it right, but 'twas too late, for the name could never be got rid of in the parish. 'Tis very unfortunate for the boy."

"It is rather unfortunate," replies Bathsheba.

"Yes. However, we soften it down as much as we can and call him Cainy. Ah, pore widow woman! She cried her heart out about it almost. She was brought up by a very heathen father and mother, who never sent her to church or to school and it shows how the sins of the parents are visited upon the children, mem."

Alastair Petrie comments on this in his book 'Releasing Heaven on Earth'. Under the title 'Generational Stewardship' he says, "Through procreation and the subsequent act of being born into this world, children inherit the ways of their foreparents. This means that sin and defilement become generational".

Psychologists Henry Cloud and John Townsend – both Christians – bring it right up to date in their book 'Boundaries'. Talking in the context of conflict within families they say, "These patterns are not new, they have just never been confronted and repented of. These patterns run deep. You begin to act automatically out of memory instead of growth".

Cloud and Townsend then talk about how to deal with these problems, "To change," they say, "you must identify these 'sins of the family' and turn from them. You must confess them as sins, repent of them, and change the way you handle them". Flame's recipe is very much along these lines, although it emphasises also the need to forgive our forebears.

~

Flame's belief – founded upon seeing the Lord heal in this way on many occasions – is that the Lord normally heals destructive behaviour patterns by going to the origins of the problem. Team members find it helpful time and again to ask if the problem is one that has history within the family. The difficulty may be one of a tendency to tell lies, it may be of quarrelsomeness or anger. Adultery or other sexual sins are areas that frequently come up. Addictive behaviours are regularly ones brought for healing. No matter what the difficulty, the person seeking ministry may well say, "Oh, yes, my father had a major problem there, just like his dad". Jacob of Genesis fame would certainly have done so – though whether he ever acknowledged that he had a problem in the truth and lies area is an open question.

It is helpful in itself to the person concerned to recognise what has been going on but the team member will then suggest that he should acknowledge the destructive tendency to the Lord, repent of it and forgive the earlier members of the family who have introduced the problem into the family line. This is the root and branch solution. The person caught up by the bad behaviour has come to see where the problem has come from, has taken responsibility for his own part in it, obtained the Lord's forgiveness for himself and has forgiven his forebears who have made him susceptible to it.

Says Jan Ransom, "Personally I know that I had huge strongholds of addictions in my family and I knew I was vulnerable in this area myself. In 1993 I attended a conference and was delivered of generational addictions. I do know I have been healed of this but still have to be careful that I am not addicted to food!"

At a leaders' conference in Boroboro in Northern Uganda Archbishop Henri Orombi recognised the truth of this teaching. On the day following the teaching he declared, "I took the sword of

54

the spirit yesterday and cut myself free from my polygamous father. Polygamy always sows division and conflict in a family".

The Boroboro conference was one at which this teaching seemed particularly to ring a bell with delegates, and to act as a catalyst for healing. Among those healed was another clergyman. Jan Ransom vividly recalls, "Canon Milton Otto Olima was convinced of this teaching when he realised his family had a curse on them. He broke the curse and told me he was healed".

Rosemary Piercy recalls the godly pastor in Burundi who was unable to achieve his potential. "He confessed the witchcraft on his family line and then found he was free of self-condemnation." Another pastor struggled with unclean sexual thoughts to such an extent that he felt that he was being visited by demons at night. He confessed adultery on his family line, and this was a major factor in his healing.

In January 2013 a team went to Ezo, a town of about thirty-three thousand people in the southeast of the Republic of South Sudan.

On the first day they taught on generational sin – the tendency for one generation to repeat the wrongdoings of its forebears. At the end of the day the Bishop's Chaplain went to the small local hospital to visit his seriously ill aunt. The teaching had really caught hold of him and he took the opportunity of the visit to preach on it to the thirty or more patients. Every single one grasped the teaching. Each confessed and forgave the sins that had come down their family lines.

The Chaplain went again to visit his aunt the following evening and was immediately assailed by the medical staff who asked, "What did you do? Yesterday all the patients slept and received some healing. It had to do with your teaching".

The scene now moves to the last day of the conference, a Monday – though time and dates matter little in Africa, even today. The Flame team was summoned to the Commissioner's office. The Commissioner had heard of the miracles that had taken place both at the hospital and during the conference.

"Please will you spend ten minutes teaching my staff," was his request.

On the steps outside the Commissioner's office the staff assembled and Jan spoke on generational sin, the teaching that had made such an impact earlier in the conference. At the conclusion of her talk she asked the team members to go round the staff one by one, laying hands on each of them. They reacted like the hospital patients: they confessed and forgave ancestral sin, which had passed into their own generation.

Jan asked the question, "Has anyone been healed?" There was an immediate response. One person said all-over body pain had disappeared, whilst another said his hernia had been healed, and still another that his impaired sight had been fully restored.

The Lord can heal physical problems, as well as mental trauma, and sometimes the key is to look back at where problems started.

7

Hammer and Nails

Flame Diary for Burundi visit, 2010: In both Matana and Buye many spoke of having suppressed their problems and experiences to find peace. People repeatedly testified that when they allowed these problems to come to the surface and chose to face them with God and then to forgive those concerned, not only did they experience deliverance, deep emotional healing and peace, but they felt better physically; stomach ulcers and chest and shoulder pains had gone. Many testified that they had gone to the root of their problems for the first time.

*"Bear with each other and **forgive one another** if any of you has a grievance against someone. **Forgive** as the Lord forgave you."*

(Colossians 3:13)

*"See to it that no one falls short of the grace of God and that no **bitter root** grows up to cause trouble and defile many."*

(Hebrews 12:15)

A wooden cross is at the centre of the stage with a supply of red, poppy-like paper discs alongside it. After teaching on forgiveness there is a queue of conference delegates, each taking the hammer, as their turn comes, and each hammering a disc into the cross. Each disc represents a hurt remembered and someone whom they have chosen to forgive for inflicting that hurt. Often delegates hammer several discs onto the cross to signify their decision to forgive several people and several hurts.

This scenario is played out at every Flame conference. It became a standard feature of ministry as a result of the visit to Borneo of Jan Ransom and Maggie Bradford in 2002. Maggie describes the cross as "a unique and powerful symbol" of the forgiveness available to those who believe, as a result of Jesus volunteering his life on the Roman cross in exchange for ours. Jan comments that, "God gave me a tool to help people apply forgiveness in a practical, physical way".

She goes on to explain how it helps the teaching and why it is only a tool. "We used it very effectively in Borneo and it was clear that people found it helpful to nail their forgiveness to the cross. But we went to one church in Sarawak where the leaders weren't happy with the idea of a visual aid and we couldn't use it. We were concerned that people would not respond to the forgiveness teaching without it but, at the end, people flooded forwards and lay flat on their faces, forgiving people for hurts they'd received."

There was also a time on a parade ground with the Sierra Leonean army where it was not possible to use the cross. The soldiers were simply invited to 'hold' those they needed to forgive in their fists, then raise and open their hands and let them go as a symbol of choosing to forgive. Remarkably, this was soon followed by the sergeant major and the troops breaking into dancing and singing their praise to God.

What did Jan and Maggie learn from this? "The lesson was helpful," says Jan. "Anything is possible with God so you don't need to rely on aids. It is the Word of God that convicts. We realised that if we were ever challenged about it again we could be confident the teaching itself would have the anointing on it."

One member of a Flame team recalls the effect of the forgiveness teaching on a delegate at a conference in Gulu in Northern Uganda, about 200 miles from Kampala, "I prayed with an elderly lady whose three sons had been killed by the Lord's Resistance Army (LRA). Later I watched as she shuffled up to the cross at the end of the forgiveness teaching and selected three red discs and carefully hammered them onto the cross". She testified later that she had found a measure of freedom. Flame's belief is that this will have been merely the start of a process.

In 2009, Pesto came to the Flame conference in Lainya, a town in South Sudan which had been heavily bombed and shelled by the Khartoum Government, as well as being a target of the LRA. He was unable to raise one arm above his head. As he told his story later, his education had been curtailed because his parents could not afford the fees. Because of this he felt bitter towards them. The Khartoum Government had killed his extended family two years earlier. As if he had not suffered enough, both his sons had been brutally murdered by the LRA three months before the conference.

Pesto's bitterness knew no bounds. He heard the teaching on forgiveness but initially could not bring himself to act on it. However, two days later he made the choice to forgive parents, Sudanese Government and the LRA – an act of great courage. The result was spectacular. "Immediately his arm was healed and he could not be held back from giving his testimony in the church and in the marketplace where we were preaching. It was a man transformed," said Jan Ransom.

Unforgiveness has been described as "taking poison and waiting for the other person to die from it." Psychologists, Christian or secular, agree on the centrality of forgiveness in restoring wholeness. Much respected Christian counsellor, Selwyn Hughes, who founded Crusade for World Revival, made much of it and said that as many as ninety per cent of those he counselled found healing, some from mental health problems, through forgiving.

Being hurt is a fact of life. Whether we are of African, European, American, Australasian or Indo-Chinese decent, we will suffer hurt at the hands of others from time to time and even the most saintly will inflict hurt. The question is not whether we will be hurt but how we react to the hurt and to the person inflicting it.

Teaching on forgiveness is always a key theme in Flame's work, no matter what other teachings are given. Forgiveness is at the root of healing, at the root of reconciliation and at the root of our relationship with Jesus. Unless we forgive others we cannot be forgiven ourselves. Our Lord was absolutely frank about this:

> 'For if you forgive other people when they sin against you, your heavenly Father will also forgive you. But if you do not forgive others their sins, your Father will not forgive your sins.'
>
> (Matthew 6:14-15)

So important to Jesus is our forgiveness of others that he instructed us to deal with forgiveness issues before attempting to worship him. We are to leave our gift at the altar and, he told his followers, *'first go and be reconciled to your brother'* (Matthew 5:24). Only then are we to go back to the altar to offer our gift of worship. Sometimes, surprisingly, the brother to be forgiven is ourself. Rosemary Piercy recalls a lady in Burundi who realised this, forgave herself and was instantly healed of stomach problems. Rosemary comments, "If God forgives our sins, who are we not to do the same?"

Eric Lomax was tortured most brutally by the Japanese as a prisoner of war. His experiences were told many years later in his book 'The Railway Man' which was made into the film of the same name. He found his life transformed in coming to a place of forgiveness. Thirty-five years or more after the war he had discovered that his Japanese tormentor, Takoshi Nagase, was alive and working, apparently as a tour guide, on the railway that Lomax and his fellow POW's had been forced to build.

He had gone back to the site in Thailand where the torture had taken place with the aim of confrontation and revenge, carrying a knife for the purpose. He discovered that Mr Nagase was involved in reconciliation work, having recognised the evil of the murder and brutality that he and his colleagues had inflicted. At the end of the film they talk. Nagase says, "I am sorry, so sorry. I do not want to live that day any more". Lomax, played by Oscar-winning actor Colin Firth, replies, "Neither do I. I cannot forget what happened. I assure you of my total forgiveness. Sometime the hating has to stop." The two men became close friends as a result and remained so until Takoshi Nagase died in 2011. Eric Lomax died the following year at the age of ninety-three.

How far Mr Lomax's decision to forgive was influenced by his tormentor's contrition is an open question, but there is no doubt that forgiveness was a big step forward in his own healing. His comments sum up what forgiveness is all about: a decision of the will and a wiping out of the debt, in spite of the memories.

Northern Ireland peace campaigner Gordon Wilson shows forgiveness at its truest, given with neither hint of contrition from the offenders nor even an acknowledgement on their part about what had happened. "I bear no ill will. I bear no grudge," said Mr Wilson on national television. This was his response just a few hours after the killing of his daughter Marie and his own injuries at the hands of the IRA in that organization's appalling bombing of the Enniskillin Remembrance Sunday service, on 8th. November 1987. In contrast to the norm in Northern Ireland at that time, he opposed any reprisals by the loyalists and went on to campaign actively for peace, even meeting with the Provisional IRA in his quest to stop the Troubles.

Gordon Wilson typifies real forgiveness. The model Katie Price, often called 'Jordan', shows what forgiveness is not and how lack of forgiveness can lead on to bitterness. In an interview in The Times Magazine in June 2013 she said, "I'm a Gemini and I forgive but I never forget. If I want to get someone back, I will get them back. Even if it takes years. I can't help it. I believe in karma. And when I do get them back I love that feeling of satisfaction. It's revenge."

Does she really forgive? Clearly not – for true forgiveness is giving up thoughts of revenge and judgement. It is handing over to

God the right to judge in his time and his way. It is a choice, made possible because we are human beings and not merely instinct-driven animals. But it is an expensive choice because it flies in the face of our natural reactions.

Jordan is right in one thing, though: she distinguishes between forgiveness and forgetting. Forgiveness sets the scene for the memories to start to fade and for the bitterness within them to subside. Without forgiveness there will be no end to the bitterness and the memories will always have power over us.

Roy Godwin and Dave Cook write about forgiveness in their book 'The Grace Outpouring' which recounts the remarkable things happening at the Welsh Christian centre, Ffald y Brenin, "I asked a lady if there were abusive people she needed to forgive, reminding her that it is a costly thing to do. When we forgive those who have hurt us we relinquish our right to vengeance. We are not saying that what they did doesn't matter any more, and justice may still demand a response, but we are saying it is now God's concern, not ours."

'A brother offended is harder to win than a strong city and contentions are like the bars of a castle,' was one of King Solomon's timeless proverbs (Proverbs 18:19 NKJV). He meant that it is extremely difficult to get close to someone harbouring unforgiveness, and that the person who won't forgive locks themselves into an isolated cell of their own making. When people do forgive, though, the results are often life-changing, just as they were for Pesto. The results – the blessings to the person forgiving – are often as major as the hurts are deep. There is a real self-interest in forgiving from the heart.

Esbon, a 69-year old Rural Dean in the Episcopal Church of Sudan, based in Nzara, carried around with him a knife and a club, the latter bearing the teeth marks of his beloved wife. She had been battered to death with the club by the LRA and Esbon was intent on revenge whenever the opportunity arose. In human terms, who could blame him? It was not just the inner man that was hurting: since the killing he had suffered chronic pain in his back and shoulders. His role as Dean was significantly impaired.

At the Flame International Pastors' Conference in Nzara in 2010 he chose to put aside the knife and the club and to forgive the LRA. Team members prayed for him. Instantly the pain disappeared and Esbon ran round the conference hall, before doing press-ups in front of the team and delegates. It was an elegant testimony to the thorough-going healing he had received from Jesus, but more was to come. When Flame returned to Nzara in 2011 they found Esbon full of vim and vigour. He was running an agricultural training programme for the pastors, to enable them to develop vegetable plots sufficient to provide food for their families and for the most marginalized in their communities. As if that was not enough, he was putting in a ten-hour day on a large allotment plot of his own.

~

In writing about forgiveness, pastor and speaker John Bevere adopts the language of debt that Jesus used in his Parable of the Unmerciful Servant (Matthew 15) and in the Lord's Prayer. "We construct walls when we are hurt to safeguard our heart and prevent any future wounds. We become selective, denying entry to anyone we fear will hurt us. We filter out anyone we think owes us something. We withhold access until these people have paid their debts in full. We open our lives only to those we believe are on our side."

In the Parable of the Unmerciful Servant each servant owed something and was chained to the creditor because they could not repay. In teaching the Lord's Prayer Jesus used the phrase "forgive us our debts as we have forgiven those who are indebted to us." It was – and is – very appropriate language because forgiveness breaks the chains, releasing not just the offender but the person hurt as well. Forgiveness means dropping our demand for repayment, even if that is no more than wanting an apology or an acknowledgement that a wrong has been done. Our progress in the process of forgiveness can be marked by asking the questions: Do I still want something back from this person? Do I feel that this person still owes me something? When we truly forgive – when we forgive without strings – we are free to walk into the future, but until that time not only have we been hurt but we have been under the control of the offender.

It is significant that, in acting out the Unmerciful Servant story as part of the forgiveness teaching, Flame teams have found that its powerful message overrides all difficulties of culture and translation.

~

Mark Leakey, Chair of the Flame International trustees and who comes from missionary stock, recalls the testimony of Edith, a Rwandan Tutsi, widowed as a result of the 1994 genocide. This was particularly poignant for Mark who had grown up alongside Edith's brother Oswald: he had been killed during that terrible genocide. Edith had cried every day for the past fourteen years and cried through a large part of the conference.

"Edith had been forced to watch as her two daughters were raped and then cut to pieces by Hutu killers; later she had to watch as a Hutu priest killed her husband. She had cried every day for fourteen years for her lost family; also she could not worship in a church pastored by a Hutu priest," recounted Mark.

"At the end of the conference, the team and delegates linked arms in a large circle in the church. The delegates were singing beautiful Kinyarwanda hymns; many of us were weeping. A Hutu priest, Anastase, who not been involved in the genocide and who had been instrumental in setting up the conference, broke out of the circle and knelt in the centre of the group with his hands raised and with tears streaming down his face. He confessed the sins of his fellow pastors who had been involved in the killings and asked forgiveness. Then Edith too broke out of the circle and came and embraced Anastase."

It was a powerful moment of reconciliation between Tutsi and Hutu. For Edith herself it marked a new beginning and she was even able to act as translator as another widow told her own harrowing story.

Edith gave her testimony later in the conference. She told how she had just experienced her first tear-free day since the genocide and went on to say, "I thank God I was always willing to forgive those who approached me for forgiveness – like the Christian who killed my auntie, but those who never asked me I felt did not deserve forgiveness. But this week I have heard differently, I have learned forgiveness. Blessed are the peacemakers. We must forgive to receive forgiveness. My team members helped me. I discovered that we are more blessed when we forgive those who have not repented. I had bitterness and hatred for the pastor who killed my husband. Every time the pastor in my church, who killed my husband, preached I walked away. I considered him dead. I was not expecting my attitude to change. Also I had bitterness and hatred towards the Council of Churches who signed the agreement of peace. I did not see God as love, but I see it now. God is able to give me peace."

As the story of Irishman Gordon Wilson shows, the need for forgiveness and the release it brings are as great in the developed Western world as in the troubled continent of Africa. With forgiveness comes freedom, as though invisible chains, which link people to the past and stop them moving into their future, have been broken. And with freedom usually comes joy, as Pesto, Edith and countless others who have experienced Flame's ministry, have found. Bitterness, too, starts to dissipate: it can only be released through the act of forgiveness. People can start to see and live a future. "I have come," said Jesus, "that they might have life and have it to the full" (John 10:10).

As Eric Lomax said, "Sometime the hating has to stop". Without forgiveness it cannot.

Bishop Alapayo of Rumbek had no doubts about the healing nature of forgiveness. Whilst addressing troops in a barracks on the banks of the Nile in December 2007 he mentioned it twice. On one occasion he said, "The teaching on forgiveness has transformed me. I have been doing this but now I do it with confidence. We forgive our enemies and hand them over to God". On the second occasion the Bishop addressed the troops he said that the Flame teaching had been a blessing to his pastors and parishes. He had often preached about God forgiving us but had now recognized, in a new way, the necessity to preach about the need for us to forgive those who have offended us. He had been very ill with malaria and depression not many weeks before but the teaching had restored his life.

~

This chapter started with words of St Paul and has included words of Jesus himself but let the last word in this chronicle of forgiveness go to two ladies who attended Flame's 'Victims of Rape' Conference in the Democratic Republic of Congo in 2013, and who took seriously the words of Jesus in Matthew 6:14-15:

> *"We will forgive the rapist because the word of God says if you do not forgive those who hurt you, you will not be forgiven. We will obey the word of God."*

~

Suggested further reading: Eric Lomax' book 'The Railway Man' is a worthwhile and moving read. It is a measure of his healing that he was able to share his experiences, a thing most men of his generation were unable to do.

Gordon Wilson later wrote a book, with journalist Alf McCreary, about his experiences, entitled 'Marie: A Story from Enniskillen'. His obituary in The Independent is on the Internet and is worth reading. For readers interested the link is: http://www.independent.co.uk/news/people/obituary-gordon-wilson-1588729.html

The quote from John Bevere is from his excellent book, 'The Bait of Satan' (Charisma House Publishing). Those wanting to consider the issues raised in more detail will find this book a good starting point. He writes out of his own experiences of hurts received, how he failed to deal with them at first, how the Lord turned his thinking and how this radically altered his relationships.

8

Free to Live

"The beginning of fear is the end of faith".

-George Mueller

Flame's Burundi Diary, April 2005: "Joy had been living with a lot of confusion and fear. Many questions had been answered and she would be leaving the conference a changed person, trusting the Lord a lot more."

The fear of the LORD is the beginning of wisdom, and knowledge of the Holy One is understanding.

(Proverbs 9:10)

"There is no fear in love. But perfect love casts out fear, because fear has to do with punishment. The one who fears is not made perfect in love."

(1 John 4:1)

Nzara, Republic of South Sudan, 2010: There is an air of hopelessness pervading the town. The LRA has been very active in the area recently and, as a result, the townspeople are too scared to sleep in their homes at night. They prefer to go out into the forest to sleep because of their fear of the LRA's thugs coming to rape, kill and kidnap. However, a town full of fear at the beginning of a Flame conference became a town with hope at its end, with people staying in their own homes at night and going about their normal business.

And yet what had changed? At the end of the conference the LRA was as vicious in its vile and random attacks as it had been at the beginning, so the danger was no less real. Was Flame's teaching perhaps encouraging the people of Nzara to live in unreality? Was it perhaps unintentionally increasing the danger to them?

These are valid questions, very much in Flame's mind, and this chapter will attempt to provide answers.

~

Fear comes to all of us at one time or another: it appears in many different shapes and sizes, some good and godly, others the exact opposite. There is the 'fear of God': a healthy respect for our God that motivates us to do things his way. This is the 'beginning of wisdom,' as the writer of Proverbs puts it, and it is indeed very good and very godly. Then there is the fear that, when faced with a car bearing down on us, causes adrenalin to pump, which in turn causes us to take almost instantaneous avoidance action and so avoid injury. This is good and godly. Likewise, the fear is completely justified which causes our African brothers and sisters to run when attacked by the LRA. Just as right is the fear that causes villagers in the Nuba Mountains (the disputed dividing line between the two Sudans) to run into caves and clefts in rocks when they see or hear one of Khartoum's Antonov bombers approaching. Sadly, this is a common occurrence.

On the other hand there is the fear that paralyses us, that makes us play safe all the time and that simply debilitates. Examples are fear of failure; fear of spiders or of confined spaces. This kind of fear often causes physical symptoms, particularly chronic digestion and stomach problems. It is extremely difficult to overcome this sort of fear, but Flame believes it is basically unhealthy and ungodly. It believes it springs ultimately from lack of trust in our loving heavenly Father, who is involved intimately in our lives and wants the very best for us.

On occasion, a fear that starts as real and healthy lingers long after the reason for it has gone and it may even intensify. Someone bitten by a dog may develop a phobia of dogs, which, in extreme cases, prevents them leaving their home. Someone involved in a minor crash in a bus may become paranoid and refuse to travel by bus ever again because of a belief that there is bound to be a crash. A godly fear becomes a controlling and ungodly one.

It is also helpful to recognise that we use many different words for fear that may mask the real issue. Brenda Schwarz, Flame International's Training Officer, identifies nine 'fear' words: anxiety; worry; tension; panic; apprehension; shock; timidity; terror; and phobia. She comments that, "They all represent separation from God".

Val Batchelor has prayed with many people suffering from fear, and comments on how it is often hidden. "It is often linked with trauma", she says. "People do not always speak it out as fear. It's a part of the trauma, and fear comes in on the back of trauma. People who have suffered one traumatic event fear that something similar will happen again. Testimonies of sleeping peacefully indicate that they have found the peace of Jesus replacing the fear."

Trauma as a result of fear can arise from any number of circumstances. Whilst working in Uganda, Flame came across a man who was traumatised as a result of a lion leaping over an open truck in which he was travelling and brushing him as it went by. There are innumerable women in Democratic Republic of Congo suffering from Post Traumatic Stress Disorder (PTSD) because of rape and the fear of its repetition.

Pastor Joseph, a Sudanese, talked of his own fear and the consequences of his healing from it, "I received inner healing at the conference. I live in fear and my heart races as I sleep but in my small group I shared and when we were out in a circle and I was able to express my pain and the tears flowed. I felt relief in my head. Now I have slept!"

Buye, Burundi: March 2010. At the end of the conference Celestine talked of his experiences. Due to the war he was fearful, and things kept coming back to his memory. For the first two nights of the conference he could not sleep. After prayer in the small group he slept well and heard a voice telling him not to fear anymore. "I stretched and felt I was completely relieved. I arrived at the conference feeling fear and as I stand here I feel released. I also had suffering in my side, and I now feel free and in peace." This is just one of a number of testimonies contrasting inability to sleep before ministry with an undisturbed sleep pattern afterwards.

Val Batchelor's experience also shows the variety of things that cause fear, though some of the fear factors for Africans are strange bedfellows to those of us in the West. Here, fear of failure is very common, as is fear of not passing exams for many teenagers, but in Africa there is also often a fear of not being able to complete schooling. Such a fear may seem trivial compared to the fear of attack by the LRA or of aerial bombardment by the Khartoum government's planes, but it is nonetheless real and needs to be taken seriously. Val says, "When you delve you find deeper fear arising from generational stuff. There's fear of a father having to go away to work, a fear of losing a parent. Where a father has been killed an uncle will provide for the children but there is a fear of the uncle dying too and, if he dies, there is huge loss and fear".

The testimony of Stephen in Rumbek, Sudan, in September 2005 shows fear arising from circumstances Westerners might once have found hard to understand, but which has become real with the advent of Ebola. He told how, when he was seventeen years old in 1991, his mother died. He was the last child. Nobody was willing to bury her because of the sickness she had encountered. He dug the grave, starting at four in the afternoon, digging in fear and working all night. Finally a Christian lady came and helped put his mother's body in the grave. Stephen described fear of seeing the dead body and of the sickness, and also his fear that, if he died of the sickness, nobody would bury him. But, after ministry, "fear lifted off me," he said.

~

"Perfect love casts out fear" – but fear seems to hang on grimly in many of us. It makes many people miss out on their full potential, preferring to stay in an unfulfilling rut rather than risk something new. It can paralyse us, preventing us from doing anything at all and, at its worst, causes immense psychological damage.

Fear was unknown in the Garden of Eden until the Fall, that moment when the eyes of Adam and Eve were opened after eating the forbidden fruit, when they became self-conscious, realising they were naked. "I heard you in the Garden," Adam told the Lord, "and I was afraid because I was naked; so I hid." It was the moment at which the world became a hostile place, when human beings became vulnerable and the possibility of fear became a reality.

Talking about fear, well-known and respected Christian leader and speaker, Christine Caine, who also heads up the 'A21' organisation combating human trafficking and slavery, says that, "Without a doubt, fear is the thing that cripples and immobilizes people more than anything else. In fact, while researching the topic of fear, I learned about literally hundreds of different phobias that affect people's lives every day".

She goes on to say that "Fear paralyzes us, thus destroying our effectiveness, and it is not a respecter of persons. The truth is, we all have things we are afraid of. If we are to truly step into our destinies, then we must decide that we will not allow fear to rule us".

"Fear is the major driver of human behaviour," says Jan Ransom, based upon her years of ministry into emotional wounds and mental trauma. "There is fear which is, at best, only semi-rational: the fear of a tiny speck of dirt; the fear of enclosed spaces or its opposite, the fear of the world outside of home. But," she says, "For people who have lived with the fear of massacre, or life under communism, fear is totally rational and real."

Jan cites as examples the Rwandan genocide of 1994 when Hutus lived in permanent fear of their Tutsi neighbours (or even their Tutsi pastors) turning on them with machetes, guns or clubs. She cites the fear of moderate Tutsis who killed their Hutu friends out of fear of themselves being slaughtered by the radical Tutsis if they refused. Many moderates were killed by their own people for just this reason. "For those who have seen genocide, there remains the fear that the hatred which inspired it is still there, under the surface, and could break out at any time."

Real fear in communist countries arises because people know there are informers, who may even be among their friends, in the pay of the secret police. There is the ever-present fear of the nighttime knock on the door as a consequence. The fall of communism has not allayed that fear. For the people of Armenia, for example, there is the knowledge that the KGB still operates in the country. In the communist era they learned not to trust one another, because an apparent friend might actually be an informer, and that fear remains, blocking relationships.

Rosemary Piercy tells of an Armenian lady to whom she ministered on a Flame trip. "She had seen her son murdered by a contract killer. Her greatest fear was that her son might not have given his life to Jesus; she experienced great release when she felt reassured by God's prompting that this had happened."

Where fear is present there is no peace and no joy. But Flame takes seriously the biblical truth that perfect love can cast out fear. It has seen people set free from fear.

~

Before going to Sierra Leone in 2003 Jan had been praying about what subjects were most important for the team to teach. "One morning I woke up with an absolute certainty that fear was one of them," she says. "Since then, I have discovered that fear is a dominating spirit wherever we travel because of the effect of war, genocide and conflict. It's essential that we teach against it to set the captives free."

Flame's teaching centres on enabling delegates to recognise fear for what it is and to see where it stems from. They are encouraged to ask themselves questions: Is my fear godly or ungodly? Is God big enough to deal with my fear and my fearful situations?

Flame encourages delegates then to confess the fact of fear and to repent where they have allowed Satan, rather than Jesus, to control them; to forgive, if what others have done to them is at the root of fear; to deal with any ungodly emotional links with others, if those are at the heart of the issue; to confess and release God from blame if, as is often the case, they blame him for their problems; and, finally, to release the fear to Jesus, asking him to deal with damaged emotions that stem from the fear. They also learn that some fears do not go overnight. It may need a considerable amount of time in which they learn to "renew their minds" before they feel completely free.

~

So there they were, Moses with hundreds of thousands of Jews – the 'Israelites' as they were then called – standing facing the Sea of Reeds. The elite forces of Pharaoh were coming at them from the rear, intent on genocide. The Israelites were trapped, cut off from any hope of escape. There was terror and panic – except for Moses, their leader, who calmly proclaimed. *"Do not be afraid. Stand firm and you will see the deliverance the Lord will bring you today. The Egyptians you see today you will never see again"* [Exodus 14:13].

And so it was. The water rolled back, the Israelites went across on dry ground but when the troops followed they were drowned as the water flowed back to its normal place.

But turn back the clock a year or two, and precisely ten chapters of Exodus. This same Moses is in the desert, talking to God who has given him the job of returning to Egypt to lead God's chosen people out of Egyptian slavery and into Palestine's freedom and plenty. He's the best candidate for the job. By a quirk of upbringing he's been brought up at the Royal Court, given the best education there was to be had. He knew the right people and, in particular, knew

Pharaoh. Moses, however, is not enthusiastic and seems anything but the leader-in-making of one of the great liberation movements of history. In reality, he is scared witless by the job offer – a poisoned chalice if ever there was one. He's wriggled and turned, using every argument and excuse he can think of to get out of it, and God has patiently answered each. In fact God is now losing patience with this man of destiny.

Moses' final gambit is nothing if not brazen and honest: *"Pardon your servant, Lord. Please send someone else"* [Exodus 4:13].

He might easily have added (and was almost certainly thinking), "I'm frightened. I don't much like my sheep-minding job, but it's much better than dealing with those grumpy Jews and an Egyptian government that tolerates no dissent. So, if it's all the same with you, Lord, I'll stay here thanks."

Somewhere along the line, however, Moses made a transition from this immobilising fear to courage and action. That transition was the key to him fulfilling his God-given life work.

Jan Ransom sheds light on how such transformations come about. "I believe it is the whole programme of Flame teaching which brings healing. After individuals have taken the rights of Satan out of their lives, as we teach forgiveness, generational sin, deliverance, freedom from fear and emotional healing, and after they have confessed and forgiven, the Spirit is free to heal without blockages. We rarely pray for physical healing until the blockages are removed. Many are healed after Satan's rights are removed!"

Scripture does not tell us about the process which transformed Moses but it likely that it involved some of the things that have transformed people coming to Flame conferences.

~

So we come back to the questions raised at the beginning of the chapter: is Flame actually putting people who live in the midst of real danger – people living in conflict zones or the women of Democratic

Republic of Congo who face rape for example – in more danger by its teaching?

Flame is careful to distinguish between godly fear and its ungodly counterpart, and recognizes that a godly fear can get so exaggerated that it becomes ungodly. The fear the people of Nzara had of the LRA was well justified. On the other hand Jan recalls a churchman in the Nuba Mountains who would not leave his home because of a fear of snakes. They are an issue in the region but normally it is the snakes that are afraid of people, showing it by scuttling off to safety. This man, however, was consumed by fear. "We delivered him of the spirit of fear," Jan recalls, "and he knew he'd been set free. Ungodly fear cripples and stops you doing things. He retained a healthy respect for snakes but was able to resume normal life, even going out at night." This gives the clue to the godly effect of Flame's teaching: it enables people living in difficult conditions to live a normal life whilst still taking sensible precautions.

This contrasts sharply with the attitudes of the LRA soldiers in the early years of that organization. They were taught that they were invincible, so did not even bother to carry weapons. Consequently thousands died, forcing the LRA to re-think its strategy. Wrong teaching led to wrong actions and death. Right teaching, plus sensible action, leads to life.

Fear could easily have enveloped Nehemiah as he and his fellow Jews rebuilt the walls of Jerusalem in 445 or 446BC in the face of opposition from non-Jews. Nehemiah's opponents tried their best to frighten him and his people by threatening to report them as rebels to the Persian king, and by talk of armed invasion of the city. Nehemiah was having none of it, refusing to be frightened and putting backbone into his fellow countrymen. But the threat of violence was real so he took sensible precautions by posting guards day and night. The attack never came.

Val Batchelor says that healing from fear results in strengthening of the spirit and clear sightedness to make right assessments and apply practical measures. "Trauma leads to lost hope," she says, "whilst healing leads to hope restored, the spirit strengthened, trust in God, and progress in the destiny he has prepared."

~

Suggestions for further reading: Christine Caine's international A21 anti-slavery organisation's website is at www.thea21campaign.co.uk

9

Restoring Relationships

"One young lady's attendance at church and house group was patchy and she suffered from many illnesses. One moment she was very much in love with the Lord Jesus and desperate for his help and presence in her life, whilst at other times she exhibited doubts and indifference in her faith, and even hostility to her Christian friends. After some lengthy prayer ministry sessions, the story of sexual abuse and enforced occult involvement (witchcraft) emerged. Once she was able to forgive her abuser, and particularly his witchcraft, we could pray to cut the ungodly emotional link with him and she was delivered of many evil spirits relating to the witchcraft as well as the abuse. After further emotional release she went on to be free to love and worship the Lord and to be stable and consistent in her walk with him. She received much in the way of physical healing."

[Wendy Whitten, Flame International's
Missions Co-ordinator]

'After David had finished talking with Saul, Jonathan became one in spirit with David, and he loved him as himself.'

(1Samuel 18:1)

Weddings are such wonderful occasions, aren't they? I'm really looking forward to this one because the bride and groom are both good friends of mine. Ah, here we go! The Wedding March strikes up; the bride is coming up the aisle to meet and marry the Man of Her Dreams. Doesn't she look fabulous in that white dress and veil? It's strange though; there are ghost-like figures behind her who seem to be attached to her by ropes. It's as though she is towing them behind her and being pulled back by the weight.

Oh, one of them is her mum. I know her very well. Very controlling, very manipulative is that lady and if she says jump the bride will always jump. The two of them are thick as thieves and always have been. You wouldn't have thought the bride had ever left home really, judging by the time they spent in each other's homes even whilst she was married to her first husband. It really irritated him. Mum would be there when he arrived home from work and he even had to take her on holiday with them.

There's a man I recognise too. It's a guy she lived with for a while before her first marriage – Jack, I think his name was. I don't know how true it is but they reckoned he was involved in séances and that sort of thing. What I do know, though, is that she was never the same after they started living together. She was potty about him – and broken-hearted when he walked out on her. I don't think she ever really got over that.

There's her friend Jennifer. They were very close for years, right from early school days. When she met Jack, Jennifer dropped her like a stone: Jen and Jack had had an affair at some point so I suppose she was jealous. At any rate they've never spoken since – but I think the bride secretly misses her.

Ah, well, there's the bridegroom, lucky man, waiting at the front to greet her. They've not wasted time, you know. They've only known each other a couple of months. Half a minute, though. There appear to be some shadowy figures attached to him too. This really is intriguing. There are several girls he had a fling with. I don't even know their names, but then he always was a bit of a ladies' man.

Oh, and there's his father. Now that's ironic. His dad is tied to him now, yet he had no time for him as he grew up. Even when he was there, he did nothing but criticise, no matter how hard his son tried to please him. I don't think the bridegroom realises it but it affects everything he does. Always trying to please, always defensive, always wanting praise and approval. It makes him very touchy. Must be very difficult for a wife to live with.

Do you know what? I'm beginning to have serious concerns about whether this marriage has any hope of succeeding. I wonder if I should say something when the vicar asks whether anyone knows of any good reason why they shouldn't be married...

~

Life is all about relationships. God saw that Adam was lonely so he created Eve to be his companion. Father, Son and Holy Spirit are in relationship with each other and, when human lives are in godly order, they are in relationship with God as well as other people. Of course, relationships don't always run smoothly, and what Jesus did on the cross was ultimately all about reconciling us to God and us to each other.

The Old Testament contrasts the relationships of Rebekah and her younger son Jacob with that of David and Jonathan. The one is good and godly whilst the other is evil and ungodly.

The discreditable story of Rebekah's control over Jacob is told in Genesis 27. She is determined that he, not Esau, will have their father's blessing despite the fact that by rights it should go to the oldest son. And so, learning of Isaac's plan to bless Esau, she instructs Jacob to go to the butcher for some best-quality meat, which she will prepare for him to give to Isaac before Esau gets back from a hunting trip. His mild protests at the deception and risk involved go unheeded. "My son," she says, "let the curse fall on me. Just do as I say." And so he did, despite realising her scheme was wrong. Carrying it through led to the total disruption of the family.

The great King David appears to have had relationships involving both bad and good emotional links. His relationship with his wife Michal, the daughter of Saul the previous king, started well and ended badly. There was genuine warmth characterising the bond initially. Michal warned David of a plot by Saul to kill him but Saul then unilaterally broke off the engagement, marrying her off to Paltiel. Later, as the price of peace, David demanded her back, and she was forcibly taken from Paltiel who *"went with her, weeping behind her all the way"* (2 Samuel 3:16) until sent home by the Army Commander. It seems that a genuine and good emotional link had been forged between Michal and Paltiel. Perhaps this was why she and David were unable to build a healthy relationship afterwards.

In 2 Samuel 6:20-23 we witness a major row between them, with Michal berating him in public for his conduct. The passage finishes with the very sad comment that, *"Michal daughter of Saul had no children to the day of her death."* Perhaps the explanation was simple: the two came nowhere near each other after this incident. Perhaps, too, the existence of the good emotional link with Paltiel was a major factor. However, many commentators suggest it was the result of the damning judgement Michal made upon her husband in her comments.

David and Jonathan, on the other hand, enjoyed a relationship that saved David's life on at least one occasion and enabled him to take his rightful place on the throne of Israel. It was life-giving, whereas Rebekah's domination of Jacob and David's estrangement from Michal were life-sapping.

The problems of these ungodly links continue into modern times and, although there will be emotional difficulties, equally important are the negative spiritual and mental effects which occurs when one person is dominated in some way by another; ungodly links are not simply emotional.

Bob Ferris and Terry Collier, the central characters in the famous 1960's sitcom 'The Likely Lads and its follow-up, 'Whatever Happened to the Likely Lads?', epitomise the problems of relationships which become out-of-balance. Set in rapidly changing Newcastle-on-Tyne, Bob and his wife Thelma are social climbers, whilst Terry, Bob's best friend of many years' standing, is a stereotypical Geordie no-hoper, locked in the past. Thelma suffers constant frustration. Terry exerts his powerful, but unseen, grip on Bob to pull him back into his old ways, whilst she tries to progress towards middle-class respectability, epitomised by the new, semi-detached suburban home they have bought.

Coming right up-to-date, the television soaps, with warring relatives and problematic friendships, show that the problems are as strong as ever.

The soaps, like the wedding scene that started this chapter, are not real-life stories. The wedding scene is based on the drama Flame uses in its teaching on relationships to epitomise the need to be healed, and to break free from the past. But, real or not, it and the soaps illustrate scenes that are played out countless times daily in real life in all parts of the world.

Birgitte came to one of Flame's Ugandan conferences. Her parents had died when she was very small, and her uncle and aunt, who treated her cruelly, using her as a slave rather than a member of their family, had brought her up. To escape this she married when very young, but her husband also abused her. After she had given birth to five children in six years her husband left her to have an affair with her sister. This left a number of ungodly links to be cut – those with her aunt, uncle, husband and sister not to mention others who had mistreated her. She received a measure of healing when this had been done.

So many people live lives truncated by bad past relationships. Parents who fail to nurture their children with love or who are abusive, manipulative or controlling, inevitably leave their mark on their children's ability to enter fully into life. Involvement in the occult causes issues. Past relationships, especially sexual ones, prevent people moving freely into the present and make it more difficult for new relationships to succeed. Rape (sadly always a feature of warfare but now a standard weapon in some parts of the world) and human trafficking wreck the lives of countless women and children. The unfolding scandals of abuse in children's homes show that the victims pay a lasting price for the perpetrators' moments of perverted pleasure.

In Sierra Leone Flame teams came across girls who had suffered Female Genital Mutilation (FGM), which has only been recognised in the West for the dreadful abuse it is in very recent years. Rosemary Piercy, a mother of two, a former trainer and veteran of at least sixteen Flame missions, was on the team and recalls that, "We found how important it was for the victims to not only forgive but have Jesus deal with all the ungodly ties between them and the perpetrators – otherwise they continued to be bound by fear."

In Uganda, as in many other places, Flame encountered instances of witchcraft, which, although many western minds find it hard to grasp, cause real harm. Rosemary Piercy prayed with a girl whose problems apparently arose because of her deceased grandmother. The young lady said that on the same day each month the grandmother would "fly" into her room, taking the girl and subjecting her to physical and spiritual abuse. Rosemary comments that, "The ministry to the girl involved breaking the relational links with the grandmother. The change in the girl was astonishing," said Rosemary. "She went completely limp and for a time we were very worried. However, by the next day, she said she was feeling far better and her expression had changed completely; the fear seemed to have gone. You just have to go with these extraordinary events and pray like anything."

Such people are truly captives to the past. It is just as though there are invisible, heavy chains binding them and making it impossible for them to move forward. They are in the position of a horse tethered to a stake that enables it to graze only within the circumference set by the length of the tether. The lovely green grass beyond is visible but unattainable – until someone releases the tether. Examples from Flame's first decade of ministry make this clear.

The small African republic of Burundi suffered genocides in 1972 and 1993, with hundreds of thousands of killings. Peter had fled to Tanzania, like many of his countrymen, to escape the mayhem, and had spent much of the following twenty years living in refugee camps. Eventually he returned to Burundi, only to find that the government had given his house to another family – perhaps understandable in a situation where it was not known when, if ever, the original owners would return.

Peter's mother was encouraged to go to court to get the home back. The result was unsatisfactory from everyone's point-of-view. It was simply an order that the two families should share the house. As a result, Peter's mother and children turned against him, because they believed he could have done more to get the other family out. Peter became bitter and angry towards both his own family and the new one. Once he had forgiven everyone concerned, and Jesus had cut all the ungodly soul ties between him, the rival family, his mother and his children, he was a changed man. This did not change a messy situation, but it gave Peter the upper hand, and great peace, in that he now knew that God would lead him 'in all righteousness'.

In a completely different context was a young, Japanese student in Paris who was overwhelmed by guilt as a result of the atrocities her countrymen had perpetrated in World War II. Eric Lomax gives an example of just how barbaric these were in the 'The Railway Man'. As the Japanese overran Singapore they took the Alexandra Hospital, the main military hospital. They "had massacred the doctors, nurses and patients, even on tables in the operating theatres. Survivors were dragged outside and finished off with bayonets".

The young woman's problems were therefore well founded in many ways. They came out during a weekend of ministry that Flame conducted in an English church in the French capital in the autumn of 2009. She was distraught. It seemed that she identified the problems closely with her grandparents, so team members encouraged her to forgive them. From there, the ungodly aspects of her links with them were severed. She left the church a much happier person.

Neither the problems Peter encountered nor those the Japanese student faced are what the Lord wants for the people he has created. Jesus described his mission by saying that he had come *"that they may have life and have it to the full"* (John 10:10). He also described part of his mission as one *"to proclaim freedom for the prisoners"* and *"to release the oppressed"* (Luke 14:18). Jesus' heart went out to those hurting people. Flame International has tried to follow in his footsteps by bringing his healing to those whose lives are mired in the past.

~

Hrazdan, Armenia, November 2013: Nora came to the Flame conference. There were many sad, care-worn faces, especially among the women, but she stood out both because of the sadness she wore on her face and her drab, gray clothing, including a gray headscarf, which she would not take off. At first sight one or two team members had an impression of a Muslim lady but it was not so. Her story was of the death of her husband in 2003, the death of a daughter three years later, followed by the death of a sister in 2009. She lived in permanent mourning and in imminent expectation of the death of yet another close family member though, in truth, all were perfectly healthy. Her daughters were not allowed to laugh within her home. It was a place of sadness and hopelessness.

Jan Ransom's heart went out to Nora and she spent much time alongside her, listening and ministering. Nora repented of the self-pity that had gripped her. "She was delivered from grief, death, sickness and infirmity, and pain," said Jan. "We asked the Holy Spirit to go in. She took off the headscarf but put it on again when she went home, which caused us some concern. But the next day she was the first to arrive at the conference and there was no shroud, no headscarf." On the following day she came to the conference sporting a multi-coloured scarf given to her by a team member, although she immediately took it off.

Most remarkable of all were Nora's comments to Jan about what had happened and the comments of one of her daughters. "When I went home last night I missed you. My emotions kicked in for the first time in ten years." On the following Saturday Nora's daughter said joyfully, "Mother is laughing. We're allowed to pray. Our lives have changed."

Ten months later Flame was back in Hrazdan. Although the conference was particularly for leaders, Nora came back on Day Three. She was clearly a changed woman, wearing a floral, coloured top and with a broad smile and relaxed manner. She was anxious to tell her story – indeed once she started talking she couldn't be stopped, even to allow the translator to catch up. The gist of her story was that life had changed for the good and permanently so. Her daughter was with her and confirmed the change in her mother, even producing a portfolio of photos of her mum wearing all sorts of brightly coloured outfits. The daughter herself was determined to go on the mission field.

~

Whichever country Flame goes to, it is normal to find people who are struggling in their family relationships. Very often the cause is a controlling parent, though it could as easily be a controlling, manipulative husband or wife. People will talk of feeling fearful, angry, rejected, maybe rebellious, or crushed deep down. They may say they are unable to make decisions for themselves or are unsure of themselves, their desires, their opinions, and their path in life.

Flame's ministry is to lead them to forgive the person who is controlling them, to ask Jesus to cut the ungodly linking which results from the controlling behaviour and to return to each person whatever unseen part of them has lodged in the other. There has often been a spontaneous release of emotion. The team will normally be led to pray for deliverance from all the spirits of fear and control that have affected the person concerned through this ungodly area of what otherwise may be a good relationship. Of course, if the relationship is ongoing he or she will need counsel on how to stand up in a godly way to the control. The team will do this, and many people have come back a few days later testifying that they are able to stand up for themselves, that the power over them has gone and that real, loving relationships are springing up.

What is wanted is to get rid of the ungodly aspects of a relationship in order to allow the godly aspects room to grow and thrive. Val Batchelor puts it at its simplest and clearest when she says that, "Godly linking brings the blessing whereas ungodly linking brings enslavement. It is the ungodly links we ask Jesus to break, and we ask Jesus to strengthen the Godly links."

However, there are occasions when all spiritual links, both good and bad, need to be broken if the person concerned is to break free of the past. It is not unusual for people who have suffered bereavement, or whose spouse has walked out on them, to continue to be completely anchored into the relationship. No doubt there will have been both good and bad links but the bond is so strong that all of them have to be broken.

Rosemary Piercy recalls a widow coming to a conference, ostensibly for ministry because of physical ailments. "We could see that she was suffering both in her mind and emotions. Initially, we asked Jesus to break the ungodly links with her dead husband, but with little apparent result. This was early in my ministry experience and I then realised that we should ask Jesus to break all links. As we did so a strong voodoo spirit literally arose up in her and, after some struggle, she eventually broke free and was filled with joy."

There are, too, relationships that are inherently and wholly wrong. If, for example, the person coming for prayer is still involved in an adulterous relationship, the only way the ungodly bonds with the third party can be broken is by the person concerned repenting and breaking off the relationship: he or she will need loving, ongoing support to achieve that, but Flame's experience is that with the breaking of the ungodly links comes greater strength to make and maintain the break.

Flame's experience also shows time and again that past sexual relationships cause present problems. Perhaps this is not surprising: *"For this reason a man will leave his father and mother and be united to his wife and the two will become one flesh"* (Genesis 6:24). This bonding happens whether the couple is married or not.

Often there is a cocktail of problems causing the ungodly bonding. One lady poured out her story of how her husband had been having an affair with a woman who was involved in witchcraft. She had cried out for many years for the Lord to set her free from the defilement that came to her via her husband's sin. Although there was still the good and godly linking between her and her husband, as she forgave him for his lies and adultery, there was prayer that the Lord would cut the ungodly element of the ties between them. This was followed up by prayer asking Jesus to deliver her from the unclean spirits of her husband's sexual sin as well as the spirits of witchcraft that had come to her via her husband and his mistress. She knew instinctively that this had been the case.

In less than half an hour the Lord restored her through the ministry of listening and prayer. She was set free to continue to love and worship the Lord and to pray wholeheartedly for her husband's salvation.

~

Jan Ransom is very clear about the deep changes that can come about in someone's life as a result of breaking ungodly links. "It has immediate effects," she says. "If you cut the ties with someone who has abused you in some way there is no longer a spiritual linking with him. It's a major tool in setting captives free. We see as a result that we can do deliverance we couldn't otherwise do."

Jesus was equally clear in saying he had come to set captives free. He does that in many ways but always wanting to go to the root of the problem. He deals with the disease rather thzn just its symptoms.

Very often the root is enslavement to the past caused by wrong relationships. Flame's experience is that Jesus can, and does, deal with that by breaking invisible and ungodly bonds when they are brought into the light by the person concerned acknowledging their existence. Val sums it up by saying, "We know that ties are powerful spiritual links and breaking them is part of Jesus' cutting people free. But they are always dealt with in conjunction with confession, forgiveness and repentance in whatever the circumstances happen to be. They form a part of a significant series of events and the healing comes from the whole thing, including the prayer for healing of the soul and spirit, and any associated deliverance."

As the stories told in this chapter show, the healings have been real and their effects both immediate and dramatic. The chains to the past are broken and people are set free to enjoy a more abundant, fruitful life in tune with the destiny God has for them.

Lieutenant Colonel (Ret'd) Jan Ransom, MBE founded Flame International in 2003 and continues today as its Director.

Brigadier (Ret'd) Val Batchelor, CBE takes time to talk with a Mission Aviation Fellowship pilot before heading off into South Sudan.

A Flame International team commits their onward journey to the Lord at the Mission Aviation Fellowship base in Kajjansi, Uganda.

At the centre of Flame's work is its Christ-centred teaching. Its training materials are translated into local languages and resources are provided to enable those trained to go on and train others.

Following the training, small groups of church leaders practise their new skills and minister to one another before returning to their churches.

Jonathan Liggins helps to demonstrate the power and strength of unity. Wherever they go the Flame teams use drama to illustrate their teaching and to bring much needed humour into difficult situations.

Maggie Liggins leads a ministry workshop for women in Armenia where, after the fall of the Soviet Union, they have seen large numbers of men abandoning their families to pursue work in Russia and Europe.

In a act of forgiveness for those who have hurt them, conference delegates nail red discs to a cross to symbolise their decision.

Bearing the burdens of those affected by war takes it toll on rural church leaders in Burundi, who are often also carrying their own grief.

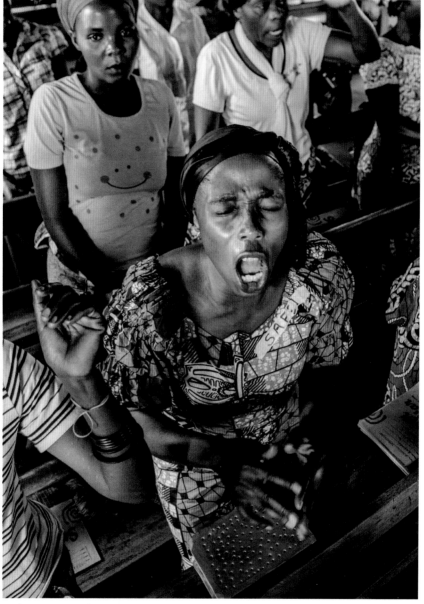

Saffi pours out her heart in worship during a special conference run for victims of rape in Goma, Democratic Republic of Congo.

A young people's meeting in Armenia was packed after the youth heard what was happening among their older relatives at the Flame International conferences, and saw what God was doing in their lives.

Volunteers come from all walks of life to serve on teams overseas and in the UK. When an outcast of society has their hands washed by a team member it can transform how they respond to ministry.

Although the tough physical conditions and dawn till dusk ministry can take its toll on even the hardiest of young people!

The Father's love is often best expressed without words.

This image of Sarah, who witnessed a mass execution by the Lord's Resistance Army in South Sudan, won 1st prize for Gareth Barton and Flame International in Restored UK's 2013 photographic competition in London.

The military have always been close to the heart of Flame, and teams always seek out opportunities to extend their teaching into the army barracks, often ministering to hundreds of soldiers at a time.

Brother Yun (the Heavenly Man) regularly tours the UK with Flame International and Back to Jerusalem, calling people back to Jesus.

The tours also raise the support needed to place Chinese missionaries from the Back to Jerusalem movement into South Sudan, in partnership with Flame International.

Bringing God's healing to hurting and traumatised communities in the wake of conflict, abuse and war means that the future looks bright for the next generation.

10

Fit to Grow

"Following Cleansing of the Land teaching last year rains came. People believed that this year more food would need to be purchased, but the land has been fertile and the food did not have to be purchased. I even prayed over my own land last year and this year it has yielded all I need. My storehouse is full. Last year I had to buy seven sacks of maize."

[Archdeacon Joel: Kajo Keji Conference
September 10th 2010]

*"Do not make idols or set up an image or a sacred stone for yourselves, and do not place a carved stone in your land to bow down before it. I am the LORD your God. ...If you follow my decrees and are careful to obey my commands, I **will send you rain in its season** and the ground will yield its crops and the trees of the field their fruit."*

(Leviticus 26:1-4)

*"If my people, who are called by my name, will humble themselves and pray and seek my face and turn from their wicked ways, then will I hear from heaven and will forgive their sin **and will heal their land.**"*

(2 Chronicles 7:14)

2a.m. 12th September 2009, Kajo Keji, South Sudan: It's raining. Not just a short shower but heavily, very heavily. The Flame team has been staying for the past ten days in a guesthouse with a tin roof and the noise of the rain on the roof is deafening, making sleep impossible. By 4a.m. Mary, the team's landlady, is up and outside in the pouring rain, needing her wellington boots for the first time in many months, and planting sweet potatoes. The rain continued night after night from then on, making the ground fertile once again.

Why is this unusual? The answer is that the area has experienced severe drought for many months past, the first crop planting has failed because of this and the people are facing famine. In the morning the locals say that the rain has come because of the Flame team. The team agrees but only to a very limited extent. Their explanation is that the previous day they taught on 'healing the land', the people of Kajo Keji had responded and, as a result, the Lord had sent the rains.

The teaching had been based on the verses from Leviticus and 2 Chronicles set out at the top of this chapter. It challenged the clergy and leaders at the conference to consider the effect of having idols on the land, and the people taking part in witchcraft. It challenged them about sexual immorality. It challenged them to reflect on the effect of bloodshed on the land, and finally on broken and ungodly covenants. The team proclaimed to the delegates that, if they repented, the rain would come. They responded immediately and repented wholeheartedly.

Jan Ransom commented by saying that, "It was an amazing privilege to be with people who really took the word of God seriously".

The second potato planting did not fail.

~

Many Christians who readily accept that God can, and does, heal individuals, baulk at the idea that land can be healed or, indeed, that it may require healing. Others interpret the scriptures by saying that, in these New Testament days, God's healing of land is spiritual and

90

that it concerns the renewing of individual lives. A book on the work of Flame International is not the place for a deep, theological treatise on the subject, though suggestions for further reading are given at the end of the chapter. However, the two scriptures quoted at the beginning of the chapter indicate that land itself can become in need of healing, and can be healed. In the Leviticus verses God says, *"I will send rain in its season"* if the people stop worshipping idols. Clearly, if they don't, he will withhold the rain. The second quotation – from 2 Chronicles – is even more direct: *"I will heal their land,"* says the Lord, provided that the people earnestly seek him.

The scriptures are full of pointers in the same direction: it has been said that there are as many as 1,700 to 2,200 relevant verses. Whilst Flame's work is with people who have been in the thick of warfare and terrorism, modern counselling has recognised the concept of "mass trauma." This is a situation in which everyone in a nation at war suffers a degree of trauma, even if not combatants or directly affected by the conflict. This is just one aspect of the need for healing of the land.

~

The Earth was created by God. As if that wasn't enough, once he had added mankind as the finishing touch, *"God saw all that he had made, and it was very good"* [Genesis 1:26]. He has never given up rights to the land: men and women are merely his managers and stewards: *"The land must not be sold permanently, because the land is mine and you reside in my land as foreigners and strangers."* [Leviticus 25:23]. The Psalmist states quite bluntly: *"The Earth is the Lord's and everything in it"* [Psalm 24:1].

Joshua 10 records the remarkable calendar adjustment that took place when *"the sun stopped in the middle of the sky and delayed going down about a full day"*. 2 Samuel 12 records a major rainstorm, out of season: *"Then Samuel called upon the Lord and that same day the Lord sent thunder and rain. So all the people stood in awe of the Lord and of Samuel."*

Such was Jesus' supremacy that he was able to walk on water, still a storm and turn ordinary water into first-class wine. On God's behalf, the wild prophet Elijah was able to declare a drought in response to the appalling evil of the reign of King Ahab. 1 Kings 17:1 tells us of Elijah's words to Ahab: *"As the Lord, the God of Israel, lives, whom I serve, there will be neither dew nor rain in the next few years except at my word."* It was three years before the rains came again.

The environmental degradation caused by pollution, global-warming and the clearing of rainforests shows how the land has suffered as a result of humanity's bad management and poor stewardship of it. Romans 8 talks *of "the whole creation groaning as in the pains of childbirth right up to the present time,"* but proclaims that it will be *"liberated from its bondage to decay and brought in to the glorious freedom of the children of God."* This is God's remedy and it will happen when Jesus comes again, the time of the *"new heavens and the new earth"* foreshadowed in the last book in the Bible, Revelation.

However, this general environmental problem is not what healing the land is about, though the symptoms show what happens to the land when man puts his agenda above God's plans. Nor is it about the devastation and degradation caused by Third Millennium man's growing obsession with violence, though that comes closer. Healing the land is a spiritual issue, although, as the examples show, once the spiritual issues are addressed, the physical condition of the land improves.

The necessity to heal the land arises from the effect on land of deliberate turning away from God, the broken relationships between individuals and nations and even deliberate co-operation with the Devil. It is illustrated by the story of Cain and Abel, told in Genesis 4, which culminated in the first recorded murder as Abel died at the hands of his brother Cain. *"What have you done?" says the Lord to Cain. "Your brother's blood cries out to me from the ground. Now you are under a curse and driven from the ground, which opened its mouth to receive your brother's blood from your hand. When you work the ground it will no longer yield its crops for you,"* [Genesis 4:10-12].

The advent of sin into the world had already made farming much more difficult. Adam and Eve were told, *"Cursed is the ground because of you. It will produce thorns and thistles for you...By the sweat of your brow you will eat your food."* Cain's murder of his brother would make life even more difficult. Ground would be so unproductive for Cain that he would become a nomad, foraging for his food wherever it might be found.

As the teaching at Kajo Keji indicates, scripture points to four things that can cause land to become in need of healing. These are matters so basic to the relationship of God and man, and to relationships between people, that they frustrate God's purposes. They are matters of depravity.

Idolatry clearly prevents God taking the premier place he should have, and blinds people to the truth. It is not that we don't have idols but that they are a little more sophisticated than those of our forebears. Football teams, celebrities, music, materialism, the emphasis on me and my rights, New Age and the like may all be examples of modern-day idolatry, to say nothing of the Buddhas and Hindu effigies which have become so fashionable as ornamentation. For our ancestors it was very down to earth. They made idols of wood or stone or followed the example of the Israelites in the desert: when Moses lingered up the mountain they made their idol, the golden calf. *"These are your gods who brought you up out of the land of Egypt,"* was the chant that followed.

Exodus 33 records that the consequences of the Golden Calf episode were extreme, culminating in God saying that they could continue to the Promised Land, but that he himself would not to go with them. Their actions had severed the relationship between God and his people. Moses recognised that the lack of God's presence would be fatal. He pleaded with God on the people's behalf, and eventually the Lord agreed to go with them, though only because of his close relationship with Moses himself.

The breaching of covenants is also a matter that affects the land itself. Covenants are solemn, binding, long-term commitments between man and God or between people. They are at the basis of God's dealings with human beings. Marriage, as described in the Bible, is an outstanding example of a covenant between two people and God. As between God and man, the Bible shows many covenants, culminating in the 'covenant of grace' of the New Testament brokered by Jesus. Time and again God's Old Testament people ignored the covenants they had freely entered into with God, and the land paid a price, with drought, infertility and invasion by insects such as locusts, or even by other nations.

Covenants can, and are, also made between people and the powers of darkness. The covenant between the ancestors of the people of Kenema in Sierra Leone and the Devil has been told in chapter 5. Its consequences were far-reaching and the healing of those consequences, liberating.

Sexual sin is the third area that has an effect on the land itself. *"Do not degrade your daughter by making her a prostitute, or the land will turn to prostitution and be filled with wickedness,"* says the Lord, words recorded at Leviticus 19:29. An injunction against committing adultery was one of the Ten Commandments, aimed at protecting marriage, which, in turn, was intended to be the basic building block of society. 21st Century western society makes light of this, but so primary does God consider it to be for a healthy society that adultery, if proved, was to be punished by stoning. Jesus pointed up the importance of marriage when he said that; *"Anyone who looks at a woman lustfully has already committed adultery with her in his heart."* [Matthew 5:28]. St Paul broadened the argument in saying (as he did in Ephesians 5:3): *"But among you there must not even be a hint of sexual immorality,"* describing it as *"improper for God's holy people"*.

In western society psychologists have described our present values in relationships, not as monogamy, but as serial monogamy. Bigamy and polygamy remain taboo but many believe there is nothing wrong in having spouse after spouse, partner after partner. We would do well to consider where this belief has led our culture.

Cain's murder of Abel exemplifies the final area of man's action towards his fellow man causing defilement of the land on which it takes place. It has often been said by visitors to former Nazi concentration camps that there is an eerie quietness and lack of birdlife on those sites. Following scriptural principles this should be no surprise: the land is cursed because of the appalling bloodshed upon it.

Africa, of course, has been the focus of Flame's work so far and is a place where violence has been endemic since records began. It has sadly seen wave after wave of bloodshed, whether by King Leopold's enforcers in Congo in the 19th Century or the LRA and similar organisations today. Much of the land needs cleansing. However, bloodshed in modern times is not limited to Africa. The Middle East is riddled with it, and it is not long back that terrorism was rife in Northern Ireland. The land suffers as a result.

In a society such as Britain, where over 190,000 babies are aborted each year, we would be wise to ask what effect this may be having, not just on people but on the land itself.

~

In Romans 8:22 Paul describes what has happened to the earth itself: *"We know that the whole creation has been groaning as in the pains of childbirth right up to the present time."* Widespread healing of the land is needed to reverse this. There is no recipe that can be followed and guaranteed to produce the result. It is God himself who will do it, but he works in partnership with his people in this, as in all things. Flame International sees its role as assisting people to identify what has caused the 'curse' on their land. That done, its aim is to help people acknowledge and confess their own part in it, to repent of that and to forgive their ancestors for bringing the problem into existence in the first place. This paves the way for breaking the curses in the name of Jesus.

Typically, planting scriptures at strategic points has been Flame's way of completing the healing. Jan Ransom recalls burying a complete bible under the floor of a church that was in the course of construction. "You seal the healing in with the Word of God. It's part of the toolkit," she says. "The scripture says of itself that it is alive and active so it will remain in the land long after the paper it's written on has rotted away."

Val Batchelor is equally enthusiastic about the lasting and powerful effect of planted scripture, "It is a fact that both blessings and curses extend to families, tribes, communities and nations, and continue for generations. What excites me is that when the living and active Word of God is planted, it is a powerful blessing. It counters the living and active word planted in the land by those who seek to curse individuals, families and marriages, communities, and nations. God's Word overrides."

Ezo, Southern Sudan, January 2013: Ezo is near Southern Sudan's border with Democratic Republic of Congo and the Central African Republic. There is a Flame team here, including the Rev. Timothy Krindi, usually known as 'Timo.' His family has had to live in the Kakuma Refugee Camp in Kenya for a number of years whilst Timo himself was one of two Sudanese pastors whom Flame sponsored to do full-time training in the healing ministry in the United Kingdom.

Following teaching on healing of the land during the conference, Bishop John Zawo had led the delegates outside to put it into practice. They had blessed water and written scriptures on pieces of paper; they had gone round the boundaries of the church, with the cross; they had poured the water onto the boundaries and buried the paper containing the scriptures. They had repeated the process at the local bore hole, medical centre and other key points.

During the night, however, Timo was woken by a demon, which warned him that his family in Kakuma was under threat as a result of the cleansing of the land in Ezo. The demon said that he could not live where scriptures had been planted and would have to go back to the Congo from where he had come. Timo rebuked the demon's threat against his family in the name of Jesus. Jan comments on this, saying, "It is not our practice to speak to demons but this one overplayed his hand and gave us deeper insight into the spirit world. Demons cannot be in land where the Word of God has been planted. The paper it was written on would be washed away in time but the living Word of God would remain."

The team prayed extensively for the Lord's protection of Timo's family. All its members were fine. This rather curious incident, however, reinforced the validity of the healing of the land teaching.

~

The acid test of this teaching and ministry is, does it work?

If a man is healed of blindness it will be immediately apparent to him and to all around him. His healing is self-evident, he can see. If a woman, bent over with crippling arthritis, is healed, the fact will be written all over her face, she will throw away her sticks and walk bolt upright. If a person receives healing from the trauma of witnessing loved ones murdered, that too will be obvious, both to the person concerned and to his or her neighbours. Happiness replaces sorrow, talkativeness replaces sullen silence, the head is suddenly held high, and life replaces a living death. The miracle of healing proves itself.

It is not so easy to validate healing of land. However, Flame has many testimonies strongly suggesting that the teaching does work. Some range from the cessation of low-level communal violence to unity between churches. Most, however, talk of climatic phenomena following the teaching, as rain replaces drought, and failed, or poor, harvests give way to abundant ones. The rains in Kajo Keji lasted for many days and made the land productive again. Jan Ransom comments, "It was not a co-incidence that we were there and that the rain came; it came immediately after the teaching on healing the land. We teach at the end of every conference on this subject and this was not an isolated miracle of healing. After the local people have taken responsibility for the sin on the land, forgiven, confessed and, where sin has been repeated, repented, an act of God like this often occurs."

Byumba, Rwanda, 4.04 a.m. 14th February 2007: there is an earth tremor, felt by everyone. There is another tremor later in the week. The teaching on the 13th February had culminated in teaching on healing – cleansing – the land, which had drawn an extraordinary response from the local leaders. These included the son of the king of one of the former Rwandan kingdoms and it was he who led the repentance.

Buye, Burundi, March 2010: At the conference there was one pastor from Kiremba, some distance away, where there had been no rain for months and where people were starving. He was the only person from his area. The day after the teaching on cleansing the land, and his act of repentance, he had a phone call to say the rain had come. A month later the local bishop confirmed that the rainfall had continued. The rains came to Buye also. They were so heavy that the team could not finish on time because of the drumming on the tin roof of the church. The Lord brought His blessings to the people.

Two years later Flame was again in Burundi. "After teaching the principles of healing the land we left the room so that the delegates could decide for themselves how they were going to address the problems on their land," said Rosemary Piercy. Delegates included representatives from each of the "gatekeepers" – people with responsibility in key areas such as health, education and safety. Each representative wrote down ways in which their organisation had broken God's laws; they then decided to repent and burn the papers on which they had written. Rosemary recalled the result, "As the first paper dropped into the fire there was the most almighty crack of thunder – from a completely cloudless blue sky. God showed his approval!"

~

The result of the advent into the world of sin was the loss to Adam and Eve of the Garden of Eden, the land beyond it becoming much more difficult to cultivate, and the crop yield much less certain. Cain's murder of his brother caused his land to become totally hostile to his

98

attempts to live off it. No surprise, then, that healing the land should result in a marked increase in crop yields. The feedback confirms this, both to communities and to individuals.

January 2009, The Episcopal Church of Sudan Bible College, Debi, Nuba Mountains, South Sudan: The college consists of two straw huts, one used as a kitchen, and a tree under whose canopy the teaching normally takes place. "This was the first time Flame had been to the college," says Val Batchelor. "As soon as we arrived we noticed a really heavy spirit of death. We all noticed it and the Bishop agreed. He told us that a student had died the previous day as a result of a snake bite, and that the Principal of the College had been ill for some time, with all sorts of pains, and paralysis all down one side. He was in Khartoum for treatment."

The students were bitter as a result of the death. The team was invited to the burial and went to show solidarity with the friends, family and remaining students. Amos Kinuya, a Kenyan pastor and one of the members of the team, preached. No less than seventeen people gave their lives to Jesus in response – surely an indication of the Lord's intention to turn the situation around.

The Bishop got together the leaders, the students and the Flame team and led a traditional, but little-used, Anglican "Beating the Bounds" service, which is based around Holy Communion. He blessed water, and then the group went round the boundaries of the church land, singing and praying as the water was poured on each corner. Finally the group turned inwards to do the same at the centre of the plot. "We did it in faith," commented Val. That faith proved well placed.

The scene changes to a settlement in the Moro Hills, 50 miles south east of Kadugli, the capital of the South Kordofan region of South Sudan. The village is called Kurchi, which Val Batchelor describes as, "In the middle of nowhere. It consists of some scattered homes, a water pump and a medical centre." The date is January 2010, almost precisely twelve months after the events at the Bible College. Val is facilitating a small group at a Flame conference and recognises two of the participants from the Nuba conference. Both are pastors and both received healing so Val asks them to tell the group what has happened. In response, one of the pastors says excitedly that there has been no more sickness at the Bible College. He reckons this is far more important than the healing he himself has received.

Fast forward to June 2010. The scene this time is Kigali in the small and beautiful republic that is Rwanda. Val is once again in a small group, though not in charge of it. She recognises the young man sitting next to her. "I asked him if I was right in thinking he'd been one of the students at the Buye conference," says Val, referring to the conference there in March 2010 three months earlier. "Yes, yes," he replied. "After the conference I went back to my land and thought I'd try out the teaching." He was referring to the teaching on healing the land. "I had the most amazing crop after that – my land had been barren before. My neighbours commented on how fertile my land was."

Reflecting on these two incidents, Val says, "After what the pastor at Kurchi had said I thought that God was joining all these things together. At Kigali I just couldn't believe what I was hearing. This was God networking. He showed us fruits of our ministry."

~

Is this the hand of God, or coincidence? It was William Temple, who lived in the 16th Century, who famously said that, "When I pray coincidences happen, and when I don't they don't." That is where Flame is content to stand.

~

Suggested further reading: There are several helpful books that deal with healing land in more detail, amongst them:

- Alistair Petrie: 'Releasing Heaven on Earth'
- Russ Parker 'Healing Wounded History'
- Ken Hepworth: 'Reclaiming the Ground'

11

The China Connection

> *"Ship your grain across the sea;after many days you may receive a return."*
>
> (Ecclesiastes 11:1)

In May 2010 Jan Ransom's original vision started to become reality.

That vision had been for Flame International to minister in the Far East, although the Lord had quickly made it clear that initially he wanted it to go to the wounded people of Equatorial Africa. Nevertheless, Jan had always felt that at some stage the Far East would come into the picture again. She had found herself in tears on seeing Chinese people on the plane, as a result of which she had been given a love for them. This long-term vision stayed with her.

The reality began at the 2008 Christian Resources Exhibition at Sandown Park Racecourse, where the 'Heavenly Man,' Brother Yun, was speaking on his vision for Europe. Jan and Flame trustee Mark Leakey, a former Air Commodore, heard the talk and Jan suggested Mark should invite him to speak at a forthcoming European Military Conference. Mark liked the idea, and was instrumental in setting up the conference as part of his work with the Association of Military Christian Fellowships. He contacted Brother Yun, who accepted the invitation.

After the Conference, Mark drove Brother Yun's interpreter, the amazing Brother Taisto, to the airport, and on the way told him about Flame and its vision. Taisto's unenthusiastic response was just one word, "Right." Undaunted, Flame wrote to the organisation behind Brother Yun's visit, suggesting that maybe there was a role for Flame in his plans. Its Chief Executive, an American by the name of Eugene Bach, replied enthusiastically. Whilst on leave in America he had seen a television programme on South Sudan and had had a vision of putting Chinese missionaries into the country. This was precisely where Flame could help.

Eugene went on Flame's next mission to Sudan to see the situation for himself. His belief in the validity of his vision was reinforced by what he saw.

Flame and Brother Yun's 'Back to Jerusalem' organisation have served each other since then. Flame has helped place and settle four Chinese missionaries in South Sudan, which lies close to one of the ancient 'Silk Routes', a network of roads opened up in the Hin Dynasty in the 2nd Century BC. These routes covered four thousand miles, with the original purpose of connecting China to the Mediterranean, particularly to assist silk exports from China. The purpose of the Chinese church is to place one hundred thousand missionaries along these routes. The ultimate purpose is to place missionaries in Jerusalem, where the church started on that day of Pentecost, over two thousand years ago.

The work of the Sudan-based missionaries is partly to preach the gospel and partly to heal the sick, supporting the work by the setting up of small businesses. These, in turn, aid the development of the new nation. Flame has organised a number of speaking tours for Brother Yun in Britain in order to raise funds to support them.

Brother Yun lives with refugee status in Germany as a result of his amazing release from prison in China, the story of which is told in his inspiring book, *The Heavenly Man*. Every trip to the United Kingdom requires the issue of a visa by the British authorities because of this. His first visit was to Guildford in 2011: the visa was issued in good time and without query. Not so the following year when a nationwide tour was planned. Seemingly the application had been lost or was being dealt with in England, rather than by the consular authorities in Dusseldorf. Then it appeared it had been sent to Dusseldorf, requiring a break-neck dash by the brother from his home in Frankfurt.

All seemed well. Brother Yun had the visa in the nick of time to get back to Frankfurt Airport to catch his flight to Heathrow. But Satan never wants the invisible boundaries of his kingdom pushed back, and does not give up without a fight. This time it came in the form of a terrorist alert at the airport. Brother Yun was in his seat on the plane. The authorities apparently believed that the threat had a Scandinavian connection and were suspicious because Brother Yun carried Scandinavian stamps in his papers. They hauled him off the aircraft, which flew without him. He could not now get to England in time for his first speaking engagement.

The authorities released Brother Yun only after he produced a picture from his mobile phone showing him standing with former President George W. Bush at the White House. Such is Brother Yun's international standing!

In England emergency arrangements were made to cover the first stop on the tour, and Mark Leakey was able to pick up the Chinese evangelist at Heathrow just in time to get him to the second meeting.

The tour was a great success. The Lord exerted his authority over Satan. Not only was money was raised for the Sudan missionaries, but many people were converted and many others were encouraged to move on in their walk with the Lord Jesus. Many Chinese young people were in the audiences because of Brother Yun's background. Not content with preaching, Brother Yun moved amongst these youngsters to encourage them. His ministry is hugely anointed and they readily gave their lives to the Lord.

One man on the Flame team said of Brother Yun's ministry, "Time was of no consequence to him. He stepped down from the platform and spoke to a large group of Chinese students near me.

Within minutes many of them had given their lives over to the Lord – and then Brother Yun set about telling them how to live out the Christian faith. It was a breath-taking sight."

~

China: a Communist republic whose population, according to United Nations figures published in 2012, numbers 1.35 billion. It is now the world's second biggest economy. Its Southeastern coast is the manufacturing centre and suffers gross pollution, which is likely to mean a five year reduction in life expectancy. In many cities there is almost permanent smog, a problem that was highlighted to the world in the run-up to the Beijing Olympics in 2008.

China: a country where there has been massive migration from the rural areas to the cities, so much so that the annual return to their rural homes makes the Chinese New Year the biggest migration on the planet.

China: a place of enormous factories, which also accommodate the workers so that thousands of people may live and work in just one building.

China: a place where the food does not correspond to what we in the West buy from Chinese restaurants and takeaways: a place where every part of a chicken is eaten, its bones and feet included; where a goat's stomach is just another part of the diet; and in Beijing young scorpions on sticks are the fast food.

The Communists came to power in 1949. The BBC's Internet history of China sums up the years after the takeover by saying, "The leadership of Mao Tse-Tung oversaw the often brutal implementation of a Communist vision of society. Millions died in the Great Leap Forward – a programme of state control over agriculture and rapid industrialisation – and the Cultural Revolution, a chaotic attempt to root out elements seen as hostile to Communist rule."

It was only after the death of Mao in 1976 that China started to move forward to be what it is today, though the Communist Party continues to maintain its grip on power and puts down any form of dissent quite ruthlessly.

Following the 1949 revolution the Communists moved swiftly to expel missionaries who had laboured for years to bring the Gospel to China's people, seemingly with little to show for their efforts. It was thought that the church would simply collapse under the onslaught, and several decades passed before it was possible for westerners to find out how it had fared. An old hymn says that, "God moves in a mysterious way his wonders to perform," and what western observers found, when they returned to the country, was an underground church that was thriving. Despite vicious persecution, it was growing at a staggering rate. That growth shows no sign of abating.

Given the undoubted strength of the Chinese underground church, it is fair to ask whether there is a need in the country for an organisation like Flame. Its answer is an unequivocal 'yes'. The oppression of communism on the spirits of the Chinese people over more than 60 years, the brutal repression of dissidents, the forced abortions to restrain population growth and the persecution of the church all mean that there is huge trauma bubbling not far from the surface. Ministering to this kind of hurt is the reason for Flame International's existence.

Flame has set about strengthening its relationships in the underground Church. Teams have met amazing people from there along the way, people such as Brother J, a man with a striking servant heart. He provided unstinting assistance: nothing was too much trouble for him. He is a man whose life, like that of Brother Yun, has been forged on the anvil of vicious persecution, with three arrests and periods in jail.

Teams have been accommodated in safe-houses where they are less likely to come to the attention of the authorities than by staying in hotels. They have been loaded into lorries with darkened windows in a garage, taken by their hosts to places unknown and let out again only after the vehicles are once more out of sight. They have been able to minister to small groups of bible students working in obscure locations, which serve as hidden bible schools. The healing work has prospered with diverse testimonies. A young woman said she "completely changed" after prayer, before which she was suicidal as a result of abuse and neglect within her family. A young man reported an "improvement" in his behaviour as a result of the teaching. Almost all benefitted from the forgiveness teaching. Several admitted that their inner thought lives had been problematic but that, after prayer by the team or their fellow students, things had changed for the better.

~

The Lord has already called out many Chinese for the Silk Routes missionary task and a major part of the teams' work has been to train, encourage and equip them. On one occasion they spent time with twenty-two would-be missionaries, aged between nineteen and forty-one. Some were clear that their call was to Africa, others sure of their call to mission but unclear about their destination. Several were clear that their call was not only to be missionaries but to be martyrs too – and they were full of joy, regarding it as a privilege to die for Jesus.

One young woman was already working in North Korea, undoubtedly the most dangerous place in the world to be a Christian. She faced the near certainty of beheading if discovered trying to proselytise. A second said she was called to Jordan, although she did not know where the country is. A team member recalls, "During a worship time, she received a vision of a map. Later when she looked up Jordan on the Internet, she saw that what she had seen was a map of Jordan, confirming that this was indeed the place she had seen in the vision".

Small Flame teams have been able to travel extensively within China to make contacts and assess the prospects for full-scale mission. They have been as far as Tibet, known as the "Roof of the World" because, at an average height of about sixteen thousand feet, Tibetans live at a higher altitude than anyone else. For those not used to living at those heights this almost invariably means suffering altitude sickness – and the Flame team members have been no exception. This has meant the debilitating symptoms of increasing headaches, nausea, breathlessness and listlessness and the use of oxygen in order to combat them.

The capital, Lhasa, (meaning 'the Place of the Gods') had particular effects on the teams over and above the altitude sickness. It is, of course, the hub and stronghold of Buddhism, containing the palaces of the exiled Dalai Lama. They observed adherents crawling to these buildings, grazing their foreheads on the pavement with each 'step' as they did obeisance. The impression was one of an oppressed, fearful people.

From the roof of their hotel they could see a village to the north-west which, they were told, was a burial centre: dead bodies were taken there, cut up and left on the rooftops for the birds to eat. The alternative was perhaps equally revolting to western propensities: bodies taken to a river and dumped in it as fish fodder.

During one stay in Tibet a prayer supporter sent a message of encouragement: "*I had the sense of the Lord breaking strongholds in that place, but starting with the small and weak. Today I have the sense that he is not doing it by might, but by a gentle spirit; I had a picture of someone picking at the base of a dam, made of compacted sand and gravel, with their index finger, loosening some of the material and causing a weakness that would set in motion, in time, the collapse of the dam and the release of the water behind it! I also had a picture of God cracking an egg open carefully, so as not to break the yolk!*" This backed up verse 2 of Isaiah 54, which the Lord had twice brought to the team's attention: "*Enlarge the place of your tent, stretch your tent curtain wide, do not hold back; lengthen your cords, strengthen your stakes.*"

It is fair to ask what these visits have achieved.

Relationships have been built. Reports on the trips comment several times on the warmth of the welcomes received, and the remarkable frankness of many key people. This means that there is an open door for Flame's return. One team member commented, though, that, "There seemed to be a great deal of emotional pain amongst the young Christians that we met, but it was difficult to know exactly what that was due to because of the language barrier and their reluctance to disclose these things to a translator". This is indicative of the underlying tensions felt by many Chinese and it may give a clue to the need for Flame to return.

The visits also enabled Flame to sow the seed for missionary activity by the Chinese in Africa as part of the underground church's 'Back to Jerusalem' vision. It seemed that many Chinese Christians were ready and willing to go out as missionaries but relatively few had caught the vision for Africa. Flame, with its teaching and practical experience, was able to envision them and to equip them.

Flame is committed to China. Jan is convinced that there is a role amongst the world's largest population group for Flame's trauma, prayer and healing ministry. She is certain that, one day, the doors will swing wide to allow it.

~

Suggested further reading: Readers wanting to understand the phenomenon of the growth of the underground church, and just how vicious the persecution of Christians was (and is), should read Brother Yun's classic book, 'The Heavenly Man'. More detailed is 'Crimson Cross-Uncovering the Mysteries of the Chinese House Church' by Eugene Bach and Brother Zhu.

12

Called to Arms

The Barracks of the Presidential Guard, Rumbek, South Sudan, September 2006: "These men have killed, raped other men's wives, stolen food, burned houses and committed atrocities, but they need Jesus in their lives and they have come to hear what you have to say to them. You are safe here. We will protect your coming and your going," – Welcoming words from the Commander.

~

"You shot me, you shot me," were the words which had kept ringing in the head of one member of the Presidential Guard since he made his first kill. He suffered constant headaches. After prayer and ministry he was healed.

"When Jesus had entered Capernaum a centurion came to him, asking for help. 'Lord,' he said, 'my servant lies at home paralysed and in terrible suffering.' Jesus said to him, 'I will go and heal him'... Jesus said, 'I have not found anyone in Israel with such great faith,'"

(Matthew 8:5-7&10)

"We have come from Cornelius the centurion...A holy angel told him to have you come to his house so that he could hear what you have to say...The next day Peter started out with them... While Peter was still speaking these words the Holy Spirit came on all who heard the message,"

(Acts 10)

"I will stay on at Ephesus because a great door for effective work has opened to me..."

(1 Corinthians16:9)

Lying between the A376 and the River Exe Estuary, and set between the villages of Lympstone and Exton in the lovely County of Devon, is the world-famous Royal Marines Commandos training base. Locals know it simply as "The Camp" and it produces some of the toughest, most able and most highly trained soldiers in the world. A high metal fence topped with barbed wire marks out its perimeter. On the estuary side, between the fence and the water, is Lympstone Commando Railway Station. Although nothing more than a single platform, there is a large sign saying, "Only those with business at The Camp may alight here". The entrances at both road and rail sides of the base have guard houses with sentries posted, carrying guns.

The message is simple: "Keep out".

The Lympstone base is typical of military establishments throughout the world –impenetrable to all who are not authorised. The military stands apart from the rest of us – a relatively small, self-contained world, protecting itself, and necessary to protect everyone else from multiple dangers.

One of the remarkable things the Lord has done with Flame International is to enable it to penetrate the impenetrable. He has provided unlikely ways into military bases where there seemed to be none and used Flame's ministry to turn round the lives of many soldiers. Flame can justly claim that at this point its ministry is absolutely unique. The Lord has truly "opened a great door to effective work" - but just how did the Lord open that door? And precisely what has been the effect upon soldiers?

~

Lt. Col Moses of the SPLA, the Sudan People's Liberation Army, which is the "government troops" of South Sudan, was eating with other officers when his medic, who was also his aide and close friend, entered, high on drink and drugs. Without saying a word, he placed a revolver in his mouth and blew his own brains out. "The contents of his head", as Moses later put it, spattered the blue plate from which Moses was eating. Even for a battle-hardened soldier like the Lt. Colonel this was traumatic, and one symptom of the trauma was inability to eat off a blue plate. The trauma went much deeper however: Moses felt guilty because, although drugs were strictly off limits to the troops, he knew of the medic's habit and had done nothing to stop it. In a curious, God-led turn of events, this incident became the key that opened the door into the armies of several central African countries and beyond.

The vision for working within the armed forces had its seed in the work in Sierra Leone, which has been mentioned in chapter 5. There had been a good deal of prayer, seeking to turn the vision into a reality. In January 2005, just a few days after the signing of the Comprehensive Peace Agreement that would ultimately lead to elections and the formation of the Republic of South Sudan, a Flame team arrived in Maridi in South Sudan. It was a time at which people were streaming back to their homes after years in the bush because of the conflict. The team was there at the invitation of Bishop Justin to conduct several conferences in his diocese. It happened, though, that four of his fellow bishops were there to conduct their own conference about the way ahead for the church, following the ceasefire. One of them, Bishop Alapayo from Rumbek, heard the teaching and asked Flame to conduct similar conferences for his own people. September 2005 was agreed for this.

Rumbek is the home to a large contingent of SPLA troops but the barracks was a no-go area to anyone outside of the army, or its political arm, the Sudan People's Liberation Movement – the SPLM. Even Bishop Alapayo and his pastors were barred. "Keep out" was firmly the order of the day. Getting into the barracks was therefore a long shot. However, Lieutenant Colonel Moses had bumped into the Bishop the day before the conference started and had accepted his invitation to attend what was otherwise a pastors' and church leaders' event.

The team prayed for Moses, a giant of a man from the Dinka tribe, standing at about six feet eight inches. He was healed of his trauma. He wanted his troops to experience the ministry and pedalled off furiously in search of the Commander of the barracks, having no idea where he would be. He met the Commander in the middle of a Sorghum field and, given that Sorghum grows to a height of ten to twelve feet, the meeting was no small miracle in itself, despite Moses' stature. Hearing Moses' story, the Commander readily agreed that Flame should come into the barracks for two days.

On the first day a vast number of troops was assembled: the Sergeant Major reported two thousand two hundred and eighty six officers and men. Most held their Kalashnikovs and some had machine guns. All the men were raggedly dressed and, to the military eyes of Jan Ransom and Val Batchelor, the weapons looked as worn as the uniforms; to the team members without a military background, it was an intimidating scene. Maggie Bradford, a nurse, commented with a degree of under-statement, "It was a little disconcerting. As Jan stood up to speak there were soldiers all around us, including one behind us cleaning a mud-caked machine gun". However, Jan preached the gospel and asked the men to respond. Nearly every hand went up.

The Lord continued to confound expectations.

On the second day the team arrived but found many of the troops going in the opposite direction: it transpired that it was the day for the World Food Programme to deliver and the men had no option but to get food to sustain their families. But what seemed a disaster turned out to be a blessing: the team was able to get amongst the remaining men, hug them and talk with them.

The team wanted to teach on witchcraft, but the Sergeant Major insisted that instead he should share his own experience. He talked of having obtained "charms" from the witch-doctor to keep him safe; of his conversion to faith in Jesus; and his realisation that only Jesus could in fact safeguard him as he had done during the last two conflicts. The Sergeant Major had taken off the charms and invited the troops to do the same with theirs. They responded without hesitation. Val Batchelor was awe-struck, "It was amazing. We had not taught on this subject despite the fact that we often did, but somehow we had run out of time and not done it. But here was one of their senior soldiers testifying to the sovereignty of God. Suddenly the cursed objects were being brought out to the front and put into piles on the ground in front of us."

Getting rid of the witchcraft items – the charms – was a statement of faith by the troops, and by the end of the day many had asked for baptism to signify their new-found conviction. The Bishop organised follow-up classes for them to ensure that their decisions were not merely a flash in the pan. Subsequently at least two hundred and fifty men were baptised.

Maggie Bradford described the reaction of the troops as "overwhelming." It was a wonderful ending to something that had started out unpromisingly: Flame had access to a major military base, relationships with senior military figures had been built, men had been converted and many baptised. For Bishop Alapayo there was the added bonus that he and his pastors had continuing access to the men and the barracks long after Flame had gone.

As far as Flame was concerned it was a strong pointer to a fruitful avenue of ministry. Said Val, "After that we took courage and always asked to go into SPLA barracks".

~

And ask they did. As a result Flame has been able to take its ministry into barracks in the Nuba Mountains, Lainya, Jau, Maridi and Nzara, and into military establishments in the Democratic Republic of Congo. It has not always been easy.

In May 2009 Flame was allowed to go into the Maridi Barracks but it was soon clear that there was a major credibility gap to be bridged. The Commander, Colonel Peter Gatwich Gai, called the team to his office. "He was clearly not taking us seriously," said Val. "He was playing with us." However, he mentioned that he had suffered chest pains for the past two years. "We asked if we could pray for him and God healed him immediately," said a team member. Suddenly Flame was welcome. The Colonel introduced them to his men and told them of his healing. They responded with enthusiasm.

In July 2013 Flame was to travel to Bunia, a major town adjacent to Lake Albert, near Democratic Republic of Congo's eastern frontier and a scene of much fighting and many civilian deaths. Flame made a request to go into the local barracks well in advance of the team travelling and was told they would be welcome – at a price: Flame would have to pay $1,500 for the privilege. This was turned down without hesitation but countered with a request that the chaplain to the barracks be allowed to come to the conference. The Lord did better than that. The chaplain not only came to the conference but also greeted the team off the plane. "We knew then that he'd ask us to go into the barracks and that there would be no question of payment," said Val. "On Day 2 he said he wanted us to go and he'd arrange it, and so he did."

Initially there was another problem. The Commander gave the team just 30 minutes at 7 o'clock in the morning. At 7.30 they were ordered off the parade ground for the changing of the guard but then the Sergeant Major allowed them a further quarter of an hour. It was obvious that the soldiers wanted more of the ministry so, sensing his men's mood, he then gave a further extension.

Once again, trust and relationship were being built and as a result the team was able to go in again the following Saturday with much greater time freedom. In 2013 Flame went back to Bunia. The team was welcomed into the barracks with open arms with a time slot of no less than six hours. A door for effective ministry had clearly been opened.

Yet a different difficulty presented itself in January 2010 when a team went to Jau, a town on the border between the two Sudans, where there had been very heavy fighting. It has a massive barracks and Flame had arranged to spend time ministering there. The problem was not in gaining access: it was with the morale-sapping accommodation they were given. Val Batchelor describes the barracks as a place of "total poverty; filth; rubbish; straw huts; loos open and full."

Val, Jan and Maggie shared a hut that was typical of the scene around. "We felt rock-bottom," said Val, "especially after hours of travelling. Maggie then said, "Let's start praising the Lord – he's given us beds!" Val continued, "We suddenly began to see things differently – the Lord got our hearts right."

It was not just heart conditions that changed. At that point a Lieutenant Colonel came and took them to a brand new tukul (a typical, round African hut providing living accommodation) with a brand new, long-drop toilet, total privacy and security. "It was a testing from the Lord," said Val. "In the new accommodation we were very comfy."

~

The opening to this chapter asked two questions: firstly, how did the Lord open doors into the armed services and, secondly, what has been achieved as a result? The first has been answered so what about the second? What have been the results of Flame's ministry amongst soldiers? The two are connected. Val comments incisively that, "They welcome us because they know God does the business. Once we've been in a barracks we are always welcomed back". The business the Lord does is healing, sometimes physical, sometimes mental and sometimes spiritual. Sometimes it is all three. He does it in different ways, on occasions immediate and spectacular and on others progressively and quietly.

To call any healing 'run-of-the-mill' would be to insult the God through whom it was done but there have been a number of healings which can only be described as spectacular. The ministry at Nzara, a town towards South Sudan's southwestern border, illustrates both.

Nzara's chief claim to fame is to be credited with the first known outbreak of the Ebola virus, with over one hundred and fifty people dying of the disease in the second half of 1976. Flame sent teams into its barracks in 2010 and again in 2011, when the results of the ministry in the previous year became apparent. A number of officers and men raised their hands to say they had been healed of physical problems. This was run-of-the-mill, though, compared to the experiences of some men.

In 2010 the Commander who was so high on drink and drugs that he could barely speak at all had welcomed the team, with great difficulty. "We invited him to the cross after the forgiveness teaching," said Jan, "Then two men from the team went back to his tukul and prayed with him." A year later the same commander greeted the team with big hugs. "He was overjoyed," said Val, the team leader. "There was not a trace of drink or drugs, his eyes were healed, he was overjoyed and in his right mind. He was a fit man, totally healed."

In 2010 a man had received healing from chest pains. In 2011 he was able to run with his men. It was a similar tale with a man whose leg had been healed.

The 2011 visit was one of Flame's Young Adults trips, which will be described in Part 3. A notable miracle occurred as a result of prayer by one of the young team members. He ministered to a soldier with a withered arm and a hand screwed up into a claw, the result of him being cursed by another man as they shook hands: the disfigurement had happened within minutes of the curse. The soldier was also hobbling as a result of being attacked with a machete. The soldier was able to forgive the people who had caused his impairments and the team member broke off the curse that had had such a devastating effect. The following day the arm and hand were partially better. "We prayed again," said Val. "He shook my hand as we left and could straighten it fully. We had faith for complete healing."

On the return visit to the barracks in Bunia in 2013 Val was able to say that, "We were praying for any number of soldiers who had arthritis or back problems. God was just healing instantly and suddenly they were able to demonstrate their healing." Yet one healing far surpassed these. Morris had had severe arthritis since 1986. He could hardly walk, but was just about able to work as a radio operator. Val recalls sending team members to pray with him. There was no apparent result. Then John, one of the team members, asked if he might hug the soldier – and he gave him a huge and sustained hug. John recalled that he suddenly felt the heart beat in the soldier whose upper body was healed equally suddenly.

And if that had been the end to it there would have been a fantastic miracle – Morris would have had full, pain-free, upper-body mobility. But it was not the end. Val recalls that as they got into their vehicles to leave the barracks someone shouted, "There's Morris!" He was walking up the hill from the offices towards the vehicles "with a huge grin and the light of Jesus shining in his face." Truly, a notable miracle, among many miracles, had taken place.

As all this had been going on the Commander returned with a large contingent of men from a deployment that had almost ended in disaster. It transpired that the Commander lived for Jesus. He told of a completely different miracle that had turned the potential disaster around. They had been down to their last four mortar bombs, he had prayed and believed the Lord was telling him to fire one bomb to each point of the compass – north, south, east and west. He did so and the rebels fled although the Commander's men were able to capture many of them as they ran. "God won the battle," said the Commander. Val believes it was the devout faith of this significant officer that enabled the Lord to achieve so much in healing his men.

"They welcome us because they know God does the business," says Val. The record speaks for itself. Truly, God has opened a great door for Flame for effective work in an important and unique section of the community.

13
Handing Over

Redundancy is a word of dread for many people, meaning the forced end of a job, even a career, the prospect of shortage of money and a loss of self-respect. For Val Batchelor, though, and her mission team of six in Nzara, Southern Sudan, the word had very different and very positive connotations. It was March 2011. This was the last of a series of visits by Flame teams and it seemed that the local Christians had understood and accepted the teaching well. Now Val and her team watched as two hundred of them taught and ministered to more than two thousand of their fellow Sudanese. The Bishop, who had invited the team, was also well pleased.

The Sudan work came about as a result of a "rather pathetic prayer – something like 'Lord, we'd like to go to Sudan.'" Ten days later Jan Ransom met two ladies, Kay Gouk and Barbara Richardson, whom she later described as "elderly and prayerful." They were aware of Flame's 2003 mission to Sierra Leone and told Jan of a conversation they had had with the father of a missionary who was working in Sudan. It didn't seem like a terribly inspiring circumstance, but doors opened as a result of it. Suddenly, it seemed, Flame was in touch with the Bishop of Maridi – but it quickly looked like a false alarm: another organisation was going. There was six weeks of silence and then the situation reversed. The Bishop made contact and wanted Flame to go.

Jan recalls that Flame had had to get a team together, make arrangements and start the conference within two months, no mean feat given the logistical problems of reaching Maridi. "Everything happened, and it was clear the Lord had opened all the doors we needed. We met with five bishops of the Episcopal Church of Sudan and this resulted in the start of the forty missions we have now undertaken in this nation. We only want to go where the Father tells us. This applies as much now as it did in 2003. Obedience is the key."

In March 2011 the work went on into the night. The Lord brought healing to delegate after delegate, as people forgave those who had brought chaos to their lives – killing, kidnapping and raping. But now was a time of celebration, colour and feasting because lives were being changed as delegates encountered God. People were saved; the weight of horrendous past experiences was lifted and bodies were healed: in particular the twisted limbs of babies were straightened.

The Flame team had spent two days before the convention putting the finishing touches to the training of the local ministers. They had prayed with many of them, and many had experienced the healing they would shortly bring to the convention delegates.

The physical healings were a sign of the unseen work God was doing within the spirits, minds and emotions of badly wounded people. At a session earlier in the day a bible had been buried to symbolise the taking back of the area from Satan's control. Shortly after that there had been a thunderstorm, another nod of approval from the Lord. In Britain, cloudbursts are thought of as a nuisance. In Sudan, where water is perpetually in short supply and where drought is a major problem, they are a blessing.

The team moved on from Nzara to Maridi, then Lainya and finally Kajo Keji. In Maridi a man was healed from a bad back that had restricted him for six years. A woman who had been dumb as a result of an electric shock was able to speak again. In Kajo Keji two hundred people became Christians and, for many, hope was restored, with many choosing to forgive the perpetrators of terrible acts of violence and oppression.

Before leaving for Sudan, the team had received a prophecy that the local people had started digging wells but that the team would help dig them deeper. On her return, Val Batchelor summed it all up by referring to prophecy in Malachi 3:10 where God promises that He will *"pour out so much blessing you will not have room enough for it."*

Truly he had. So much so that Flame is redundant in the area. It has handed over the ministry to the local people so that they can take on the work. It is a sad fact that the conflicts erupting in the world mean that there are more and more countries in need of Flame's ministry of healing so the end of the work in one place merely gives Flame an opportunity to open up in a new one. In Africa, for example, the Democratic Republic of Congo has now become the focus of Flame's work. The need is simply infinite, but Flame International's aim, wherever it goes, is to enable local people to carry on the ministry without Flame's help.

~

A number of common threads run through the Flame missions: going only where invited; identifying with the conditions of the local people; the main thrust of the teaching; the use of drama; the involvement with local armed forces, prisons and hospitals. But there is one more universal thread that needs emphasising in order to show Flame International's work in its true perspective.

Kampala, Uganda, March 2006: Jan Ransom, Val Batchelor and Katja Samuel are sitting at the desk of the President, Opolo Nisibambi, who is opposite them. It is quite clear from his body language that he is seeing them under protest and thinks them time-wasters. They are there through the good offices of the Rt. Honourable Grace Akello, the Minister of State for Northern Uganda. She wants Flame to visit an area in the north with her where the LRA has wreaked havoc over the last 20 years. She wants Flame to minister to the countless people whose lives have been ruined as a result.

Jan suggests they should pray. The President sees this as an opportunity to finish the meeting. Jan has other ideas. The

President prays but Jan prays immediately he has finished. "I prayed for the Holy Spirit to bless him in his governance, to bless the country and the people of the nation of Uganda. As soon as I finished his countenance changed and he realised we were for him and not against him." The President was now warm towards them, affirmed the work they were doing and hugged each of the Flame threesome. They were thrilled. Says Jan, "This was the spiritual cover we needed to do the ministry Grace Akello had asked of us." The 'spiritual cover' Jan speaks of is spiritual authority. It involves the teams accepting the God-given authority of the team leader and the leader in turn accepting the authority of those who have asked Flame to come.

Kenema, Sierra Leone, June 2006: "You have my authority to do whatever the Lord has called you to do in this town." It will be recalled that these were the words of the Chief Headman, effectively the mayor, which allowed Flame to carry on its ministry in a Muslim-dominated area that might otherwise have been hostile to its activities. They signalled the beginning of a mission that brought significant new life to both the town itself and to the townsfolk.

Bujumbura, Burundi, July 2011: Jan Ransom, Val Batchelor and Mark Leakey have flown into the country literally "on a wing and a prayer." A 'wing' because they had come by plane, following the conclusion of a mission in Bunia, in the Democratic Republic of Congo. A 'prayer' – actually many prayers – because they have come to visit the President but, despite months of effort back in the UK, have been unable to make contact with him, let alone set up an appointment. Jan, though, had felt strongly at the beginning of the year that they should see him. The visit is highly speculative.

Subsequently there is a series of God's 'coincidences' that lead to a very successful private meeting with the President, Pierre Nkurunziza. They visit a local Flame supporter by the name of Ali, and whilst they are with her the President's Protocol Officer rings so Ali takes the opportunity to broach the visit to him. The following day they visit Major General Silvestre, another friend of Flame's. It transpires that he is a close associate of the President and he promises to use his influence to set up a meeting.

Now Pierre Nkurunziza is no conventional president. He is in his second term of office and is the only president to have achieved that: several previous presidents have been assassinated during their first term. More than that though, he is a Christian and identifies with his people: Two or three times every week he goes to some of the country's many building projects, rolls up his sleeves and helps with the construction work. Ali suggested the Flame team should go to Ngozi, 100Kms away, on the following Saturday and join in the construction projects on which the President was apparently to work.

On the first project the president came into the line next to them so that they were able to make introductions as they passed bricks. On the second project they were whisked out of the cement bucket-passing line and into a private room for their much-desired meeting. There seemed much common ground. The President shared his vision for his country, Jan was able to tell him of Flame's own vision, to share what Flame had already done and to introduce the possibility of healing the land to him. The President readily took it on board. Relationships sprang up, particularly because Mark Leakey and he had both been born in Buye, had mothers who had worked in the same hospital and fathers involved together in the Anglican Church: God's happy coincidences.

Mark takes up the story, "At that point the President leaned across the table towards me. "My brother," he exclaimed. He thanked us for our work in Burundi, affirming what we were doing and in effect giving us the cover [the authority] to continue. Ali shared with him a picture she had received from God about a seed, and she believed this was for him. We finished with prayer as we all linked arms. I had the huge privilege of praying for him and for Burundi."

These episodes illustrate clearly what has always been the case. From the outset Flame has acted under the cover of those in authority and is constantly seeking to build good relationships with them. Only with those people's blessing can the ministry succeed. For Christians in Britain, brought up in the consumer culture that puts self at the centre, it is too often a question of going it alone if the church leadership does not agree. Authority is constantly in question and barely tolerated even though the Scriptures lay down a clear doctrine of submission to those in charge.

Christians in Africa would find strange this attitude of antipathy to leadership.

Flame's belief is that it can only act where it has authority. If given that privilege, it must submit to the authority of those in charge in the place of ministry, even if this results in it being unable to cover topics it would like to teach. If invited by a particular church, Flame's teams do everything with the agreement of the leadership; if invited by a bishop or archbishop to conduct training and ministry to all the churches coming under his authority then the team will only go as far as the bishop or archbishop will allow; if invited into an army barracks it seeks the authority and blessing of the camp commander. On occasion, the results of coming under the authority of a senior military figure have been quite spectacular.

Most of all, Flame wants to gain the approval of those with political clout – "the great and the good." This is not because of a desire to be part of the establishment but because the blessing of powerful people gives Flame maximum freedom of operation and authority in their country. To quote Flame's Chief Executive Officer, Jan Ransom, "It is just that it gives us the assurance that we are operating under the right spiritual protection in the nations concerned. It is affirmation of our ministry."

INTO THE SECOND DECADE

14

Then God Took Over: Armenia

"Now to him who is able to do immeasurably more than we can ask or imagine, according to his power that is at work within us, to him be glory in the church and in Christ Jesus throughout all generations, for ever and ever! Amen!"

(Ephesians 3:20-21)

Saturday, 9th November 2013. The 01.45 Aeroflot flight leaves Moscow, bound for Yerevan, the capital of Armenia. On board is a Flame International team, drawn from the United Kingdom and Norway, its purpose to conduct a six-day mission to two churches in Hrazdan, a ski resort 6,000 feet above sea level. The cabin crew is dressed in smart, dark blue uniforms with emblems of Russia – the hammer and sickle – on their collars and cuffs. Though its members are polite and efficient, smiles are in very short supply. They seem stereotypically Russian, as far as the Western European team is concerned. Like most stereotypes, this one is untrue, as subsequent Aeroflot flights showed. In reality, the straight faces are no doubt the product of the time of night.

The plane is crowded. The majority of the passengers are roughly-shaven men in their middle years, mostly dressed in drab, black leather with black caps. They are migrant Armenian workers on the way home for a break. Their appearance is prophetic of the things to come for the Flame team as it minsters to the leaders and members of Renewal and Word of Life Churches. It is also a pointer to the drab state of post-communist Armenia.

Gareth Barton, Flame International's Communications Director, was a member of the team. "There is a cloud of hopelessness over Armenia," he says. "There's no vision, the exodus from the nation is increasing, the population is now under two million – it's as though the women and children have been, and continue to be, abandoned."

~

Armenia is a country that has rarely enjoyed independence. Bounded by Turkey, Georgia, Azerbaijan and Iran, its borders have expanded and contracted and even now it is in dispute with Azerbaijan over the status of the Nagorno-Karabakh region. In the mid-1890's Armenians suffered genocide in what was known as the 'Hamidian Massacres', named after Sultan Abdul Hamid the Second of Turkey. However, in 1915 the Turks, under Kemal Ataturk, embarked on a 'final solution' in Western Armenia (which the Turks claimed as Eastern Turkey) by massacring the Armenian population. They acted with appalling brutality: the name of Kemal Ataturk and the phrase "Young Turks" are synonymous with utter brutality – and with good reason. About a million and a half died and vast numbers fled to set up groups of ex-patriots in places such as the United States. This genocide eclipsed the Hamidian Massacres in both scale and barbarity.

Turkey has never acknowledged this genocide. The Armenians remember it every year on April 24th but particularly they remembered it on 24th April 2015, the centenary of its outbreak. Flame's vision for the country is to change the heavy spiritual atmosphere for which this genocide bears much responsibility.

No sooner had the genocide finished than communism took over, giving the Armenians no time or opportunity to come to terms with their grief.

Communism is oppressive because it tries to force equality by total control. It is an idolatrous form of religion, requiring the total loyalty of those forced to live under it. It cannot therefore tolerate Christianity or any other faith that will not acknowledge its supremacy. Similarly, family bonds must take second place to the state. As in Nazi Germany, children are taught to put country before parents and to inform on their family if members engage in anything that could be regarded as subversive. Trust disappears.

The communist regime fell in 1991, but the belief systems and attitudes it engendered linger on, powerful and unhealed. Mistrust, passivity and hopelessness characterise the prevailing mood. There is no work ethic because there are few jobs to be had, and communism has taught the people dependency. Such is the despair that Armenians are fleeing the country at a staggering rate, with the population down from three million to two million in a handful of years. Men are disappearing in droves to Siberia, lured there by Russian promises of house, job and pension, leaving a population which one estimate puts at twenty seven women to one man. The towns are littered with crumbling and disused factories and soviet-era, drab, concrete residential blocks.

Armenia claims to be the oldest Christian country in the world, but there is disunity among the churches. In particular the Apostolic Church of Armenia, the major denomination in the country, has issues with the protestant and Pentecostal churches.

~

Monday 11th November 2013: The two conferences – morning and evening – start with the declaration of a vision for Armenia given to Flame team member, Jeremy Clare. The vision is of a room locked from the inside, with a fetid atmosphere caused both by the lack of fresh air and the crowds in the room. The window is dirty and closed, but the Lord intends to open it during the conferences. Jeremy tells the people, "An open window offers an opportunity to change the atmosphere before the 2015 anniversary. All Armenians, including

Christians, need to go to the open window and breathe in the fresh air and light of Christ. God will see them at the window."

He goes on, "Ask God to look into your heart where he will see what needs healing. The door represents the door to Armenia, which has been closed for a long time. Many people in Armenia have not experienced the wind and fire of the Holy Spirit. People can open the door from the inside. God says, 'I have opened the window but I want you to open the door.' Once the window is open you will find the key to open the door from the inside. When the fresh air and light comes in, the atmosphere will change and people will stop leaving."

Very quickly, as the conferences proceeded, Jeremy had a further vision and was able to tell the people that there were two keys held together on a key ring. The two keys are unity and obedience, whilst the key ring is love. All these have been in short supply in Armenia.

Wednesday 13th August 2013: The ground has been prepared during the previous two days by teaching on matters such as the roots of communism; the fall of man; the interconnection of body, soul and spirit; ungodly relational links; loss and depression; forgiveness. There has been opportunity for ministry into these areas. The teaching on forgiveness, which is always critical to Flame's teaching, has evoked a big response with many delegates coming forward to nail red, paper discs to the wooden cross, each disc symbolising a particular hurt, and forgiveness of the person who has caused the hurt.

During morning devotions the team receives a 'word' from a prayer supporter in the UK. "You are breaking generational curses of iron and steel shackles. God has given Flame a unique key for Armenia. A blacksmith is bending iron to mould it with heat. It's the heat that makes the difference." Later, as the team teaches and ministers to nearly 100 people, Jan Ransom receives a text message from a prayer supporter in England. It refers to Exodus 34:5-7 and 10:

*"Then the Lord came down in the cloud and stood there with him
and proclaimed his name, the Lord. And he passed in front of
Moses, proclaiming, 'the Lord, the Lord, the compassionate and
gracious God, slow to anger, abounding in love and faithfulness,
maintaining love to thousands, and forgiving sins...'. Then the
Lord said: 'I am making a covenant with you. Before all your
people I will do wonders never before done in any nation in all
the world. The people you live among will see how awesome is the
work that I, the Lord, will do for you.'"*

Jan quietly asks the two pastors to name the 'ruling spirits' over
Armenia. They name publically spirits of war, death, hatred,
idolatry, Mother Armenia (a huge statue towering over the centre
of the country's capital, Yeravan), rebellion, abandonment and
disunity.

Suddenly the Holy Spirit takes over the meeting. Such is his
weight that Jan has to be supported by two team members. The
pastors lead public confession and repentance of the problems. They
are like lions, roaring out their words, with the people shouting
out their agreement. They declare unity between their respective
churches, and pronounce forgiveness to the Turks and the people of
Azerbaijan.

Pastor Artavazd's wife comes forward and relates how she and
other women had come to the church day after day over a period
of ten years, to plead for the revival and renewal of their country.
They had come without shoes through snow, and had stood on cold
concrete floors, covered only with cloths, praying over periods of five
hours for a move of the Spirit. "Today," she declares, "we are seeing
those prayers answered."

The evening conference also came alive with the presence of
the Spirit. There were many testimonies of spiritual, emotional and
physical healing. One of Flame's guiding principles is that body,
soul and spirit are intimately connected, so that a problem in one
area will often explain problems in another. Invariably the team

members perform a short drama to explain this at an early stage in a conference. Several of the testimonies illustrated the effects of the oppression of communism on the human spirit, showing themselves in neck, back, chest and stomach problems. Several delegates testified to their release from these symptoms as the real issues in the spirit-area were healed.

Many delegates told of the enormous changes brought about by forgiving long-held hurts. "I had a heavy burden on my chest. I have forgiven three people (my husband, sister-in-law and brother-in-law). Now I am feeling light and free and my burden has gone," said one lady.

"I thought I had forgiven but after the teaching I realised they kept coming back into my mind," said one lady. "I thought I could forgive at home but realised I wouldn't forgive myself if I did it at home. I needed to take action and I ran to the cross. I nailed four discs! Before, I thought I was on good terms with God. But I had a desire to have more of God. I felt as though I'd lost my first love but when I nailed those discs onto the cross it felt like heaven had opened and I felt Jesus' love so close."

God was simply showing his love for his people and his joy in the renewal taking place. "I had not heard any word or revelation from God for sometime. Two people prophesied over me on Monday evening and God spoke to me directly. I heard his voice. It was the answer to my prayer." This was a typical testimony.

Knarik Saribekyan, one of the hard-pressed interpreters, gave a simple but powerful testimony, "I have been coughing at night and haven't been able to sleep properly so I've been tired. Now for last two days I have stopped coughing".

There were an equal number of testimonies from men. One spoke particularly of healed relationships. He had been estranged from his children as well as his brother. After teaching and ministry, he had spoken to his children and asked their forgiveness, resulting in father and children coming together to the conference, reconciled.

It was an astonishing day. Team member Maggie Liggins later declared, "The abiding memory of the mission for me was when the two pastors stood together in unity, asking the Lord to push back the spirit of communism and other ruling spirits over Armenia. Their prayers were so authoritative. It reminded me of Aslan roaring in the C. S. Lewis book, *Chronicles of Narnia*. The spiritual 'Winter' effects of Communism were being pushed back by the Holy Spirit, and all the delegates very soon joined in with their own prayer."

The team had expected to be back in Yerevan early enough on the Saturday to taste the rich culture of Armenia by a visit to the opera. The Lord had other ideas. The two pastors asked Flame to do a youth conference on the Saturday afternoon. This turned into a very special ending to the ministry. To the astonishment of the team members, about one hundred and seventy youngsters, some perhaps no more than eight, and others in their lower twenties, filled the hall. They were as eager to hear the teaching, as had been their parents and elders. The teaching was quick-fire but the effects were dramatic. The team was able to minister to individuals and all were offered the opportunity of coming up for prayer and blessing. Virtually all of them took advantage of the offer, coming with all manner of requests. Here was the future of churches that had been given a new start and a new heart for the Lord.

Shushan Ghazaryan, another of the interpreters and daughter of Pastor Artevazd, later summed up what had been achieved.

"So much of church is about being inward looking: Am I good enough? What must I do to become more holy? Am I different to others? It's all about what I should do for myself. But this conference helped us think, 'Hey, it's time to take your nation into your hands; it's time for action. There's a huge work to be done, to cleanse our nation, to heal the people.' It's really pushed us forward. I don't like Armenia to be associated only with genocide. Hopefully, we will have a different Armenia in the next few years."

Shushan continued, "In the past there's been a spirit of competition between the churches but that's been broken. We saw what a touching moment it was as to have two pastors holding hands and praying for the nation – we knew something was happening in the heavenly realms. So many people are now opening up to tell painful stories that have been suppressed and they are finding freedom and relating better to each other."

What comes next? "Now we have to get to work," replies Shushan. "We're surrounded by refugee neighbours who call themselves atheists after the Nagorno-Karabakh war. We can't let this be just another conference that people enjoy and let disappear off into the past without seeing a change, because there *was* a change in the spiritual realm. We have to see the change in the physical realm – in the city. We're excited. Excited and nervous."

~

Armenia is a land of problems. But there are good things happening too. "Prayer is changing this nation," says Gareth Barton. "We witnessed God's presence through the worship being brought wholeheartedly by the Armenians, and through prayer. We experienced the glory of the Lord during the meetings; there was a heaviness of the Holy Spirit which was releasing healing, powerful prayer and an anointing on all that was going on."

Another man on the team said, "In forty years of being a Christian I have never experienced worship like this. There was joy, power, expectancy, intensity and gratitude to God at a level I could not previously have imagined. In the midst of so much dreariness the people of the two churches were on fire for the Lord."

15

Double Jeopardy: Democratic Republic of Congo

"I give God thanks. The past month we were all like dead bodies…I was carrying a heavy burden and from the first day it started to go bit by bit. My blood pressure was very high: I was not sleeping well. In the group, Jesus released me and the burden has been taken away. I am now feeling fresh air waving on me – even blowing on my heart. I am feeling good now and my hope is with Jesus,"

–Adelphine (delegate at the Flame Conference,
September 2013)

The Democratic Republic of Congo: a vast country that lies roughly to the south of the immense Congo River. To its west is the Republic of Congo. According to epithets given it by the United Nations, it is "the Rape Capital of the World" and "The Most Dangerous Place on Earth to be a Woman."

It is vital to realise the reality of rape in DRC and the effect it has. Just why, for example, does Margot Wallström, the United Nations Special Representative on Sexual Violence in Conflict, use that phrase, "the most dangerous place on earth to be a woman?" The answer is that the rape of even one woman is an appalling crime but rape in the DRC is now endemic: two in five women have been victims. Horrifying though that statistic is – it is sadly only a part of what makes rape a catastrophe.

Gareth Barton, Flame's communications director and photojournalist, saw at first hand the enormity of the cost to victims of rape when he travelled with Flame to Goma in 2014. He met a young woman of twenty-five who was willing to talk of what had happened and its devastating effect on her life. When she was fourteen, and working the family plot, three men approached her. "They tied me up, blindfolded me, pushed me to the ground and took it in turns to rape me. Then I got pregnant."

This was only the beginning of her sufferings. Being raped, and especially becoming pregnant as a result, carries with it colossal stigma. This led to rejection by her family and to life on the streets. "Being out there on my own, I kept getting raped and I now have four children from that." She is still homeless and lives in an area where victims like her gather together with their children, using metal sheeting to protect them from the rain. For her, and countless other Congolese women, rape is double jeopardy.

Gareth commented on the problems faced by these women, "Time and again I heard about their concerns for the future – for them and their children. It was what lay in front that they were focussed on, not what lay behind. Becoming an outcast has enormous physical, social, emotional and spiritual effects. How will they survive? How will they stay safe? How will they find support? How are they going to find hope? How are they going to escape this nightmare? The rape is terrible but the stigma is crippling."

~

Although rape is now the major abuse facing the Democratic Republic, it is only the latest in a long line of horrors its people have had to endure. In the 1960's there were almost daily press reports of atrocities, following the grant of independence, as President Patrice Lumumba struggled to assert authority and order in a state being torn apart by tribal struggles for domination. Atrocities included the murder of missionaries. The Western powers – Russia and the United States – carried on their Cold War by proxy, with Russia backing the President and the USA fomenting rebellion under Joseph Mobutu. Lumumba was assassinated, executed by a firing squad led by Belgian mercenary, Julien Gat. Eventually, the country was renamed Zaire until a further war resulted in it reverting back to Democratic Republic of Congo.

Yet this was only the tip of the iceberg as far as Western involvement was concerned.

Africa was of interest to Europe and the Americas as the source of slaves but, once that trade was abolished, interest waned. The Anglo-American explorer H. Morton Stanley (of "Dr Livingstone, I presume" fame) brought it back into focus as a result of penetrating the Congo with an expedition from Zanzibar on the African east coast. Stanley realised there was huge mineral wealth to be had and, under the guise of benevolence, tried to persuade European governments to get involved. "There are 40 million naked people on the other side of the rapids," Stanley wrote, "and the cotton-spinners of Manchester are waiting to clothe them...Birmingham's factories are glowing with the red metal that shall presently be made into ironwork in every fashion and shape for them...and the ministers of Christ are zealous to bring them, the poor benighted heathen, into the Christian fold."

Only King Leopold the Second of Belgium responded. Under the same veneer of bringing civilisation to the 'barbarians,' he carved out a huge personal fiefdom for himself, using Stanley as his agent. Both Leopold and Stanley were as unscrupulous in their methods as they were in their ambitions. The result was a personal fortune for Leopold but cruel enslavement of the Congolese.

In more recent years, the 'Interahamwe' (the Rwandans who had been at the centre of the 1994 genocide in their own country) has harassed Eastern Congo. Fearing retribution, they fled in their thousands over the border and have since roamed the countryside, stealing, killing and raping indiscriminately. The residents of Goma, the Flame team's first stop, had finally taken action to protect themselves against the Interahamwe by forming their own militia, and had caused them to flee. However, such is the fragility of peace in the area that the militia then turned in upon itself, causing yet more deaths.

This, then, was the country and area that was the destination for the first Flame mission of its second decade.

~

"I had said yes before I thought of the practicalities," said Jim, commenting on his family's decision for him to go. "My wife and I had prayed and discussed and prayed some more. It felt right to go, and despite the current state of my family finances, I committed to travel with Flame to DRC. I had a sense that the funding would come. And this bears witness to God's provision; provision not only materially but also emotionally and spiritually."

Continuing to talk about the need for financial and prayer support, Jim said, "It provoked me to contact friends and family, some are followers of Jesus and some are not. In response I received wonderful encouragement, precious blessings and a chance to connect with some I had not been in contact with for far too long. It also enabled me to communicate something of what Flame is about and the life-changing significance of forgiveness, both within their work and also in my life and walk with Jesus.

In short, as I packed the final things into my bag the night before leaving, the last of the money I needed came in, and that included the twenty per cent on top that I felt prompted to pledge to support Flame's core costs. What an amazing blessing! Over twenty people had given something. In some ways the most exciting was the contributions of those who would not call themselves Christians – captivated by the vision and mission that Flame has in travelling to communities that have experienced violent conflict and genocide."

Flame missions are not cheap and nowhere were the cost issues more marked than in the April 2013 trip to Goma and Bukavu in the DRC. Team members have to pay for themselves. None of the missions goes to an Easyjet destination. Often there is the cost of a Mission Aviation Fellowship flight to the local airstrip from the nearest airport worth the name. There are accommodation costs and several countries charge 'exit' taxes as the price of going home.

No less than four other team members had similar stories to that of Jim. One, a doctor, was not only given the money needed to finance the mission, but was able to take quantities of much-needed drugs and equipment for the remarkable Heal Africa Hospital*. Another was able to secure a supply of bibles translated into Swahili at a very reasonable price. Not only did this allow Flame to give out the bibles, but it provided the church in DRC, which supplied them, with the finance to finish roofing its building.

~

April 2013, Goma, DRC: A city on the northern shore of Lake Kivu and very close to the Rwandan border, Goma is home to about a million people. With its lakeside position it looks idyllic from a distance but it, and its people, have suffered hugely as a result of the spill over from the Rwandan genocide and two subsequent Congo wars. In 2010 it was captured by M23 rebel fighters, but liberated by government forces two years later. If that were not enough, part of the town was inundated by volcanic lava in 1992 as a result of the eruption of the Nyiragongo volcano which left many buildings ruined, and part of the town with a ground level two feet higher than before.

Team member and father of two young children, Jim Robinson, recalls, "We walked across the border from Rwanda into Goma. I was not sure what exactly to expect, but I knew we were there with a purpose and I had a sense that God would work through us in the coming weeks."

The conference started on Monday. By halfway through Tuesday delegates were beginning to share what they were experiencing as a result of the teaching. Two pastors said they had been unable to sleep the previous night, because they were so excited by what they were learning. A lady told of her fear of a bullying authority figure. It was what she described as "harsh leadership". She had realised during the conference that Jesus was alive and the fear had been replaced by joy.

Two pastors related how they had realised that, because of Jesus, they had been given spiritual power and authority. They had come across two men and a girl on a motorcycle. The girl, a secondary school pupil, was shouting and, according to the men with her, manifesting an evil spirit. The pastors had led her to the Lord, taken authority over the evil spirit, cast it out and counselled the girl for several hours.

By the end of the day one team member, Val Batchelor, was able to say, "Perhaps one of the most impacting truths was of the need to bless. We blessed each delegate and then they blessed each other – it was very powerful! There were many answers to prayer. What we had asked for in the morning was certainly answered." A number of delegates were reporting noticeable improvements to their health: there were no sensational healings but many long-term aches and pains – joint pains, headaches, stomach pains – had disappeared.

The following day saw more of this, but delegates were also sharing deeper, inner, emotional healings as a result of forgiving and dealing with behaviours and attitudes that had come down through their families. Innocent told of a dream that summed up what was happening: he had seen a picture of himself half-dressed then fully dressed. His explanation was that it was a before-and-after picture: half-dressed was his, and his companions' state before the conference, whilst fully dressed was what they would be like after receiving the teaching.

And so it continued until the close of the conference on the Friday. Many, who suffered continually disturbed sleep because of both past trauma and fear of more violence, told of release, resulting in undisturbed sleep. One man, Eric, told of significant improvements in relationships within his family, which had been divided by polygamy, and of his hope that this was only the first fruits of reconciliation.

Jim Robinson was deeply moved by what he had seen and heard in the workshop groups in the last couple of days of the conference. "The workshops offered the space to share a painful and profound event, and to respond on the basis of God's love for us, the power of forgiveness, and the power in challenging and cutting anything not part of God's best for us. As each delegate took a turn, the others became increasingly involved and animated in offering the way forward, in putting the teaching into practice and exploring what this meant in the specific context of family, community, church and Goma.

"And what was amazing – not only the times of sharing, listening and connecting – was that we saw people physically healed. As people brought their pain to God, as they forgave, or began the process of forgiveness of those that had hurt them, so some were healed. Aches and pains were relieved, sight improved, stomach pain disappeared, grief and sorrow lifted, and sleep was better than it had been for years."

It seemed that many of the delegates were now 'fully dressed,' as Innocent had seen in his picture a day or two earlier.

~

April 28th 2013, Bukavu DRC: Bukavu has been described as "a green hand, dipped in the lake" because it is partly built on five promontories sticking out into the water. It is a city of 800,000 people on the south-eastern shore of Lake Kivu, at the opposite end to Goma. With a wonderful climate and its position fifteen hundred metres above sea level, it was extremely popular with Europeans. Bukavu's status, however, declined as Goma's grew but, like Goma, the people have suffered terribly as a result of the overspill from the Rwandan genocide. Subsequent violence included the assassination in 1996 of the town's Archbishop, and the rape of 16,000 women in one weekend, when rebel forces were given a free hand by their commander.

The Flame team had moved on from Goma to run a conference in this sad place. The pattern of the previous week repeated itself, with few dramatic healings but many people testifying to normalised sleep patterns and healing from long-term aches and pains. This was surely a reflection of the deeper healing of traumatised hearts, minds and crushed spirits. It is an indication of the danger of daily life in the DRC that no less than two delegates were attacked coming to the conference – yet both were able to tell of release from fear as the teaching and ministry progressed. One cleric, however, was healed of something more life-threatening than aches and pains: he had been sick in hospital with spleen and liver problems and severe pain if his sides were touched. He came to the conference and, after prayer, felt no pain.

The conference gave the delegates – mostly pastors and church leaders – the opportunity to talk about their own shocking experiences and to share some of the pain with the Lord. Again, the workshop groups later in the conference played a significant role and, again, Jim Robinson was deeply affected. "In many cases people made the profoundly difficult, but life-giving, choice to forgive, and we collectively prayed for God's healing power to move in them and in their families and communities. As I listened to these experiences it was hard to know how I'd respond, how I'd cope living their lives. I had nothing to offer in terms of answers or solutions. But, of course, that wasn't why I was there. As a team we came to listen, to share more of Jesus – Jesus who loves each of us, and wants to transform situations of pain and suffering. So we listened, and we prayed. We stood and cried with those suffering grief, trauma and fear. And God moved."

Of longer term significance to Flame's development was the time that Jan Ransom and another team member spent away from the conference with a dozen victims of rape. They taught and encouraged them in forgiveness, and prayed with them. The seeds were sown of special conferences in DRC, specifically for the victims of rape rather than church pastors and leaders. These seeds not only grew quickly but also bore much fruit.

~

September 8th 2013: The team were now in Aru, a Congolese town in the north-east of the country near to the border with Uganda. Shortly after they arrived Jan Ransom preached on generational sin in the Cathedral. It was evident that the drama the team used to illustrate it broke the ice and brought the teaching to life. Jan invited people to come forward for prayer. At first there was some hesitation but then they came – probably between sixty and eighty delegates. One young man confessed openly sin he had committed, and became a Christian. Another young man was shaking all over as a team member prayed for him. The young man went away calm.

There was a clear order and reverence about the whole meeting, which lasted three hours. It was evident that the Lord was at work even before the conference-proper had got under way.

The sense of expectation continued as the conference started the next morning. One man had travelled three hundred and fifty kilometres by motorbike in order to be there. Others had come between a hundred and two hundred and fifty kilometres by bus. Many of them had lost a spouse, a child or a home in the previous fighting. There was a queue at the door and delegates started singing as they were let in.

"Thank you for coming to war-torn Congo," said the Bishop to open the conference. "My hope is that every delegate will experience abundant life and physical healing as a result of it." The delegates each declared, "I love Jesus" as their opening.

The two previous conferences had seen many people receive large measures of healing in body, mind and spirit. It became clear that this one would see much more. The teaching on forgiveness caused each and every delegate to respond. Instead of red discs, they were asked to place small stones at the foot of the cross, as had delegates at the Goma and Bukavu conferences. It was a statement of their choice to forgive.

The teaching on healing of the human spirit brought a big response. Many recognised that their spirits had been crushed by the events of life and wanted to experience renewal through Jesus and through prayer. You can see people with damaged spirits in any shopping mall or High Street even in the western world: though they usually do not recognise it, the light has gone out from their eyes; there is a care-worn and heavy look about them; they exist but do not live. But, as The Message translates Jesus' words in John 10:10, the Lord said, *"I came so they can have real and eternal life, more and better life than they ever dreamed of."* He intended it for Africans, Caucasians, Jews and everyone.

Testimonies from delegates began to come thick and fast. One man talked of the crippling burden of fear of authority figures, of feeling condemned by others and a feeling of weakness. All that had gone, he proclaimed happily.

"Now I have the courage to go forward," said Georgine. She told how demonic forces had held her back, with lots of temptations around her and things blocking her, but was now liberated.

Delegates in Goma and Bukavu had talked of being able to sleep soundly for the first time in many months, sometimes years: here in Aru one lady said exactly the same, although two men said they were now not sleeping because they were so excited by the teaching and had so much to discuss.

Tsandia reported that his daughter had been critically ill in hospital and on a drip. He knew God wanted him to come to the conference so on the previous Saturday he had told the Lord, "If you want me to go you'll have to do a miracle." He had set out for the conference in faith and, when he arrived, heard that his daughter was well on the way to recovery. "It was the string of Satan to stop me receiving the teaching, but praise God that he released me to come," said Tsandia.

Samuel, a pastor and one of the translators, said, "Yesterday I was healed of a curse. Blessing is a very good word. I was healed because I used to bless people in church but cursed my children when they did bad things. I cursed my daughter when she got married and she has four children from different husbands. My second daughter got pregnant by my brother. This makes my life difficult. I do not have joy in my family. Yesterday, when I received the stone, I said to God, 'this stone represents my hard heart towards my children. Will you heal me of that.' Something burned in me and then cooled down. Now I have a new life inside with a soft heart."

Ukello said that, although he had prayed with his family, he had never blessed them. He had repented of that and, when his daughter returned from school the previous day, he had blessed her. She was taken aback at first but, when he explained how he had been affected by the conference teaching, there had been joy and laughter.

It was as the delegates had sung on the Wednesday morning to start the day, 'God is good, all the time.'

The conference ended on a resounding high with more testimonies. "I had all-over body pain but now I am healed," said one, whilst another reported that a back problem had resolved.

Rev. Samuel, the translator who had spoken of his experience a couple of days earlier, was on his feet again to tell of his experience in the small-group ministry session. He had shared his difficulties at home. "My spirit is telling me I have already healed," he told delegates. "God has empowered me to continue this work in the diocese. I felt pain in my back and kidneys going away and I believe it will now be completely healed."

Samuel's remarks about taking the teaching and healing to other people greatly excited the team because that is precisely Flame's aim. It follows the example of Jesus who knew he couldn't do it all himself and therefore concentrated on training his disciples so that they could take the Gospel far and wide.

A lady who said, "We were dead but now have been brought back to life", best summed up what had been achieved.

~

Suggestions for further reading:

Gareth Barton's comments, and the story of the young woman which provoked them, are taken from Flame's A4 publication *'Adding Injury to Insult.'* This contains stunning photographs taken by Gareth and an article by Dr Philip Lucas, which was originally printed in Flame's periodical, *'Burning Issues'* in February 2014. *'Adding Injury to Insult'* was produced for distribution to those involved in campaigning for change, such as former Foreign Secretary William Hague, but a copy can be obtained from Flame on request.

For those interested in learning more of the history of the Congo, following Stanley's initial exploration of it, Adam Hochschild's thoroughly researched and very readable book *'King Leopold's Ghost'* (Pan Books) will be very helpful. The Evening Standard describes it accurately as 'a horrifically readable history'.

For those wanting to understand the factions involved in the bloodshed, Faith McDonnell and Grace Akello give a very helpful glossary of the politics and war lords of central Africa in their book *'Girl Soldier: A Story of Hope for Northern Uganda's Children.'* The book shows the origins of the Lord's Resistance Army, tells of Grace's experiences of being abducted by it, her escape and subsequent rehabilitation. Although the so-called LRA is the best known of the private militias, there are several others roaming equatorial Africa, with the M23 being one of them.

~

*The work of the Heal Africa Hospital, and of Dr Jo Lusi, its Medical Director, is inspiring and is described in the following link: http://www.icmdahivinitiative.org/pages/dr-jo-lusi.php

16

Dreams and Visions

"My thoughts are nothing like your thoughts," says the Lord. "And my ways are far beyond anything you could imagine."

(Isaiah 55:8 NLT)

So Jesus explained, "I tell you the truth, the Son can do nothing by himself. He does only what he sees the Father doing. Whatever the Father does, the Son also does."

(John 5:19 NLT)

What lies ahead for Flame International? How will its ministry develop over the course of its second decade?

"The future of Flame International lies in the overlap between these verses," declares Jan Ransom, referring to the verses quoted at the beginning of this chapter. "We must find what the Lord's thoughts are and then obey them – and we've often found that his thinking is far beyond ours."

To illustrate that she cites her initial wish to be involved in mission in the Far East, which the Lord countered with the airborne vision of the map of Africa changing colour in the traffic light sequence. There was then the radical change that came about during the first visit to

Sierra Leone. "When we first started Flame International, we thought we were going to be ministering to women," says Jan. "However, the male chaplains in Sierra Leone asked us why the men were not receiving the ministry. This seemed to be of the Lord because, if we taught the men, the ministry would multiply." And so it has.

That, however, was merely a step along the way. The early ministry in the Democratic Republic of Congo, with its countless victims of rape, brought the realisation that the normal means of operation – conferences for church pastors and leaders enabling them to take the ministry out to their churches and beyond – was inadequate. What were needed were conferences directly for the victims of rape.

In a stroke of irony, this brought Flame back full circle: ministry to women only. Would this find the thoughts of the Lord? Would it be doing his will? "Absolutely," comments Jan. "The need stared us in the face, woman after woman who had been abused and whose life was in utter ruins. We didn't need a vision or a picture because the picture was living human beings, right there in front of us, and we have been given keys that bring healing to them."

Jan subsequently led the first of these special missions and, bearing in mind that Flame started out as a ministry only to women, her comments may be surprising. "The conference for the victims of rape was a huge learning curve for us. As we received words of knowledge it became obvious that extravagant love was required, which came from our hearts. A word suggested that if we hugged these ladies something more than we could see would pass from us to them. This is what we did; offering hugs from the front with the ladies choosing from whom they would receive this ministry. They ran to both male and female team members and hung onto us until it became embarrassing. We know The Lord was doing something special because their hopelessness turned to hope and we experienced joy like we have never seen before. We saw the Lord transform lives and it was our privilege to be part of how the Lord was working in them. In some ways we had never seen so much transformation."

More conferences for these downtrodden women are clearly part of Flame's work in the immediate future.

~

The 'traffic lights' and Sierra Leone episodes proved pivotal in the early development of Flame International. Speaking of the 'traffic lights' vision, Jan says, "I am convinced one of the Lord's plans was to help us make relationships with godly church leaders in Africa, and this we have done. I believe we were obedient to the call of God on our ministry. We now cannot meet all the requests that we receive to go to Africa but I have a hunch that the amber light is now on for Africa and we have to get ready to stop." She admits to not understanding precisely why this should be and does not think it means an abrupt end to the African work. Rather, Flame must look wider than the African continent.

"The needs in Africa are still very great but we are handing over our ministry in these nations to hundreds of pastors and leaders and it is for them to take the work forward. I believe we are being led by the Lord to the most unevangelised part of the world, which is in the '10/40 window' heading east from Israel on the Silk Routes. The needs here are even greater and the work is tougher, due to the established religions in these nations, which means we have to work underground. Maybe the Lord has been training us in Africa for such a time as this."

The so-called '10-40 window' is the area between latitudes 10 and 40 degrees. One key to it may lie in the 'Back to Jerusalem' vision of the underground Chinese Church, so powerfully projected by Brother Yun. "In 2010 we started to be impacted by their vision to put 100,000 missionaries into the countries between China and Jerusalem. This includes nations in the 10/40 window and it happened to include Sudan where we have many contacts," comments Jan. Since that time, of course, Flame has been working in partnership with Back to Jerusalem and has placed missionaries in Sudan.

Jan takes this further, "It looks to us to be part of the end-times scenario. Approximately a quarter of the world's population is Chinese and it seems that they are likely to be used significantly in respect of the return of the Lord Jesus Christ. We sense that we are a very tiny part of the Lord's plan to trumpet in his return. We are humbled to be part of this as well as excited; this is the West helping the East to go into Africa." She goes on to use a phrase that is central to her thinking and one that she often uses, "Obedience to the Lord's call is key."

China as a nation is heavily involved in the economic development of Africa, although this is probably not for purely altruistic reasons. Nevertheless, this may well add authenticity to the Chinese Church's involvement in the continent and it seems entirely possible that it will take over where Flame leaves off, with the ground prepared for it.

Jan, however, is quite clear that this would signal a new beginning, rather than an end, for Flame. "The important thing is to do what the Father tells you and for the last couple of years we believe the Father has been pointing us towards the Silk Routes and the 10/40 window. We have already established credibility in Armenia, we have travelled into China and we have a heart to go to some of the most traumatised nations in this part of the world. We have to take a country at a time as we follow the Lord's leading."

How will this happen? Jan considers that partnership with other Christian organisations is the key to the Kingdom of God coming in greater depth and multiplication. "We are being asked to travel with larger organisations in order to take the keys we have learned over the last few years to countries that we would never have dreamed of at the start of our ministry."

~

How far does Flame's future lie in practical relief work? At the Ashburnham celebration of its first decade many people spoke of the need for the healing ministry to go hand in hand with practical help so the subject has been hot on the agenda of trustees' meetings. "We see the need," says Jan, "and are very keen to see that the people we help are given practical assistance." One consequence has been a recent gift of £1,000 to the Southern Sudanese Diocese of Ezo to help Christians there set up small business projects. The fruit has already been seen, with 111 people thriving as a result of the enterprises they have started with the aid of loans from the fund.

However, at the forefront of Jan's mind is Jesus' foundational statement, made as he was shaping his ministry and before going public, that, *"Man does not live on bread alone, but on every word that comes from the mouth of God."* So she asserts that, "We have a specialist – virtually unique – ministry, and are very keen to maintain our focus. We know we will lose that if we do relief work directly. There are a number of organisations that have real expertise and experience in giving practical aid, which we don't have, so we want to work in partnership with them. It is a win-win situation because they are eager to have the benefit of our healing ministry and we can ensure relief provision for those we help without losing our focus."

This is becoming reality. In Lira, Northern Uganda, Flame has built a partnership with Global Christian Trust. This is an overtly Christian work, involving development by predominantly agricultural business projects. Jan has nothing but praise for what it does. Flame is looking at other strategic alliances to ensure that it is able to meet both spiritual and physical needs.

"We partner in order to see the Kingdom come," comments Jan. "Our partners see the spiritual warfare work we do and understand its significance." Matthew Parris of the Times, the atheist whose comments opened chapter 4, would no doubt readily agree with that assessment.

~

The future, then, lies in maintaining and developing the niche ministry of healing the broken, being alert to where the Lord may want that ministry to be taken and working with Christian relief agencies in order to ensure completeness in what is done. But it also goes beyond that.

Flame is conscious of the need to be a thoroughly professional organisation and has put much effort into this. "We are marketing ourselves as professionals in order to win the confidence of the Christian public, to gain financial support and encourage participation," comments Jan. A glance at Flame's publications will show how deep this has gone. Until recently, the organisers of the New Wine festivals offered prizes for the best exhibitors' stand – and Flame consistently won them.

It is also conscious of the need to train present and potential mission team members. In order to facilitate this it has a Development and Training Co-ordinator who runs the training, the knock-on effect of which is that local churches also get people trained in healing and deliverance. Some larger organisations have asked for the training too, which is a measure of its quality, success and relevance.

There is a particular need to train young people in the ministry to ensure its long-term viability. The comment by Sierra Leonean pastor Arnold Anthony, made as he reviewed the events of Flame's second trip to his country, rings in Flame's ears, "I'm amazed that this was done through a bunch of old, white women," he had said. Jan and the team were slightly taken aback at the time by this misogynistic comment on Arnold's part, but it was prophetic in its own way and since then nearly a decade has passed. Clearly, the future must be with the younger generation and Flame is conscious of the need to secure that future by bringing on younger leaders and team members. Already the average age of trustees is falling as those retiring are replaced.

Special missions have been organised annually since 2011 for 18-30 year olds. This is known as the Young Adults Programme – YAP – and Jan is enthusiastic about the results, "We have had three missions into South Sudan taking young adults who hope to train for mission," she says. "We want to envision them for mission and challenge their faith. This has to be the future for our ministry. Younger people need to be stretched and we hope their lives will be changed! We hope future leaders of missions will come with us, we hope one day a future director will emerge. Young adults with a passion for mission for the Lord Jesus Christ to the nations is how we see the future, before Jesus comes again. We want 18 -30 year olds ministering in the power of the Holy Spirit, seeing forgiveness, healing and reconciliation."

As if that were not enough, Jan enthusiastically expands her vision for the YAP programme. "My heart is to take radical young adults and let them experience culture, life and ministry in areas where local young adults have the same passions, lives and drive as them, but do not have the same privileges or opportunities as themselves. My prayer is that seeds for mission will be sown in the lives of team members that will never leave them, and they will never be satisfied until they are on the mission fields themselves. I pray also for the young adults in South Sudan to have mission ingrained in them."

Getting young people interested is no easy task. The present-day church is not awash with young people, a crisis to which it has awakened only in recent decades. There is not therefore a huge pool of young people from which to recruit, and Jan is choosy about who she takes. "Our problem in recruiting for YAP is that we need to be in relationship with young adults and this needs to be ongoing. They need to be discipled properly as followers of Jesus and this takes time and energy. It cannot be done just by email; it needs personal contact and relationship. This is what we strive for in getting radical young men and women on our missions. I dream of many missions populated by young people in the future."

She pauses for breath and then says simply and with excitement, "Bring it on, Lord!"

Professionalism through and through, including working with partners who are equally professional, is the right approach as far as

Jan is concerned and will increasingly underpin everything Flame does.

Ultimately, though, the future of Flame International is in the hands of the living God. "Our role," says Jan, "is to humbly serve him, to listen to what he tells us to do and to be obedient to him. We know that without Jesus we can do nothing. The walk of obedience has not been without its challenges and it will continue to be a challenge but we 'seek first his righteousness' in order for his Kingdom to come! How easy is that?"

~

Flame International's work continues at a pace. Since the Ashburnham party, teams have been going out every few weeks, either under the leadership of Val Batchelor or Jan Ransom. The reports from these Second Decade missions seem to indicate an increase in their fruitfulness and it is interesting to have Val and Jan's comments on whether this is so. They both speak with enthusiasm and in very similar terms.

Both identify the different ways of ministry evolving in recent missions: Val particularly talks of the ministry direct to the victims of rape in DRC.

Both use the word "freshness" in describing what is going on and attribute this to the increased level of prayer commitment and intercession on the part of Flame's supporters. This shows itself in the number of messages reaching their teams day by day. Val, for example, speaks of a mission to Boga in the Democratic Republic of Congo in February 2015 where, "We were getting about five scriptures, words, poems and songs every day. Simply amazing and long messages." Why were they amazing? It was "because they were so accurate and relevant to what was going on in the conferences."

Jan comments that, "As a result of the increased level of intercession and involvement, the anointing and fruit of the ministry has increased. We are seeing God impact lives to a greater degree.

We are seeing more signs and wonders but it's to do with the increase of God's presence with us."

Quite where Flame International will be working at the end of the second decade of its life is not clear but its history indicates that this will emerge at the right time and that the way in which the ministry is carried out will continue to evolve. It can be said with great confidence, however, that many, many lives will have been changed radically and for good.

~

Suggested further reading: Global Christian Trust's website is interesting and shows how it works. The site is www.globalchristiantrust.com

*Flame International is aware of only one other organisation offering similar ministry. This is 'Sharing of Ministries Abroad' (SOMA), which is an Anglican ministry using very similar teaching but rather different methodology.

Afterwords

"Going on mission with FLAME to Burundi in April 2012 gave a fresh dimension to my prayer life!

"Serving in a very different country brings home the differences in spiritual environment around the world. Africa seems to have a greater spiritual 'fluidity' to it than Europe does, with its history of enlightenment and then post-modernity, acting like layers of rock - squashing peoples' response to the Gospel. In Africa there is a different worldview: the 'spiritual' is real and to be acted upon.

"How wonderful it was to bring Biblical teaching and to see it instantly acted upon by those attending FLAME's conference-a preacher's dream! How true it is that confessing our sins to one another is literally a gateway to the power of Christ being present to heal and to deliver (James 5:16)!

"The gift of discernment of spirits isn't just about discerning right doctrine (although this is an element) - it's about understanding how and what to pray. Bringing this home to the rural parishes that I lead and serve has helped me to put the right spiritual 'prayer key' into what had seemed 'locked'.

"What is the history of your church and area? Ask the Spirit of God – and the local librarian – to show you! And see the Lord begin to shift the junk out of the way of the Kingdom's advance!"

[Andrew Chalkley is ordained in the Church of England and is Rector to five rural churches south of Bath.]

~

"It has been a real privilege for me to serve my brothers and sisters in Africa through Flame International. Ministering God's healing into such broken lives and seeing transformation take place before your eyes is such a privilege. Heavy burdens and pain from the past are lifted as God meets with his people and fills them with His Spirit and joy.

"I have many wonderful memories of God touching lives-such as the man who shared all he had done wrong in his life with a group of men in a ministry session. God forgave him and filled him with such joy that, for several days after, we saw him continually laughing and crying with tears of joy.

"What an amazing loving God we have that He should do this work in broken and hurting lives and allow us to be part of it."

[Barry Edge – Member of numerous Flame teams]